Life in the THIRTEEN COLONIES

New Hampshire

Michael Teitelbaum

children's press®
An imprint of
SCHOLASTIC

Library of Congress Cataloging-in-Publication Data

Teitelbaum, Michael.
  New Hampshire / by Michael Teitelbaum.
    p. cm. — (Life in the thirteen colonies)
  Includes bibliographical references and index.
  ISBN 0–516–24573–2
  1. New Hampshire—History—Colonial period, ca. 1600–1775—Juvenile literature. 2. New Hampshire—History—Revolution, 1775–1783—Juvenile literature. I. Title. II. Series.
  F37.T45 2004
  974.2'02—dc22

                        2004002646

1 2 3 4 5 6 7 8 9 10 R 13 12 11 10 09 08 07 06 05 04

A Creative Media Applications Production
Design: Fabia Wargin Design
Editor: Laura Walsh
Copy Editor: Laurie Lieb
Proofreader: Tania Bissell
Content Research: Lauren Thogersen
Photo Researcher: Annette Cyr
Content Consultant: David Silverman, Ph.D.

CONTENTS

✳✳✳✳✳✳✳✳✳✳✳✳✳✳✳✳✳✳✳✳✳✳✳✳✳✳✳✳✳✳✳✳

The Original Thirteen Colonies, 1775

NEW FRANCE

MAINE
(part of Mass.)

St. Lawrence River

Lake Champlain

Lake Ontario

Mohawk R.

Lake Erie

NEW HAMPSHIRE

• Falmouth

• Portsmouth
Newburyport

Salem •
Boston •

MASSACHUSETTS

Cape Cod

Albany •

NEW YORK

Hudson R.

Delaware R.

Connecticut River

Hartford •

New Haven •

• Newport

RHODE ISLAND
CONNECTICUT

Susquehanna R.

New York •

Long Island

Perth Amboy •

PENNSYLVANIA

Philadelphia •

• Burlington

Pittsburgh •

York •

• New Castle

NEW JERSEY

Appalachian Mountains

Baltimore •

DELAWARE

Ohio River

Potomac R.

MARYLAND

Alexandria •

Atlantic Ocean

James River Richmond •

• Chesapeake Bay

• Williamsburg

VIRGINIA

• Norfolk

Roanoke River

Hillsboro • Halifax •

Edenton •

Salem •

NORTH CAROLINA Bath •

Cape Hatteras

Salisbury •

New Bern •

Pamlico Sound

• Charlotte

Cross Creek •

Cape Fear R.

Camden •

• Wilmington

SOUTH CAROLINA

• Georgetown

Augusta •

Savannah River

GEORGIA

• Charles Town

Savannah •

SPANISH TERRITORY

NORTH
EAST
WEST
SOUTH

Legend

— Colonial boundaries
(The western boundaries of many colonies were undefined in 1775.)

0   125   250

Scale in Miles

INTRODUCTION

A Nation Grows
From Thirteen Colonies

❋❋❋❋❋❋❋❋❋❋❋❋❋❋❋❋❋❋❋❋❋❋❋❋❋❋❋❋❋❋❋

New Hampshire is located in the northeastern part of the United States in the region called New England. It is bordered by Canada to the north and the states of Vermont, Maine, and Massachusetts. New Hampshire has a small section of coastline on the Atlantic Ocean, but most of the state lies inland in the White Mountains.

When the first European colonists arrived, New Hampshire was home to many Indian people. Conflicts between the colonists and Native Americans would shape much of New Hampshire's colonial history.

New Hampshire's first settlers established farms and towns throughout its many fertile valleys. They gained a reputation for being self-reliant and tough. This is the story of how these colonists lived and how they helped form the United States of America.

The map shows the thirteen English colonies in 1775. The colored sections show the areas that were settled at that time.

CHAPTER ONE

The Europeans Arrive

✳✳✳✳✳✳✳✳✳✳✳✳✳✳✳✳✳✳✳✳✳✳✳✳✳✳✳✳✳✳✳✳✳✳

The First European Explorer

When British sea captain Martin Pring guided his ships, the *Speedwell* and the *Discovery*, into the Piscataqua River in present-day New Hampshire in 1603, he was amazed by what he saw. Pring could tell that people had been there, but he saw no one. He said:

> *In all these places we found no people...We beheld very goodly groves and woods replenished with tall oaks, beeches, pine trees, fir trees, hazels, witch-hazels, and maples. We saw here also sundry sorts of beasts: stags, deer, bears, wolves, foxes, lucernes [lynx]...But meeting with no sassafras, we left these places.*

✐ *Martin Pring and other explorers were amazed at the many different types of animals that lived in the New Hampshire woods.*

Pring's voyage was the first recorded visit of a European to what is now New Hampshire. He had been hired by a group of British merchants to bring back sassafras roots. People believed that the sassafras plant could cure many sicknesses. The merchants also asked Pring to find a water route across America. European traders hoped that there was such a water route, so they could use it as a shortcut to Asia and its riches. Pring took two ships and a crew of forty on his trip.

Pring did not find either sassafras or a water route through America, but he did explore some of the land that would become New Hampshire. The *Speedwell* and the *Discovery* then continued their journey. They sailed down the coast to Massachusetts, where they did eventually find sassafras. Pring headed back to England with the valuable root. The purpose of his journey was business and exploration. He had no desire to stay or settle in the new land.

Sassafras Rhyme

In the 1600s sassafras was thought of as a cure for many ills, as this rhyme from that period shows:

In the spring of the year,
When the blood is too thick,
There is nothing so rare
As the sassafras stick.
It cleans up the liver,
It strengthens the heart,
And to the whole system
New Life doth impart.
Sassafras, oh, sassafras!
Thou art the stuff for me!
And in the spring I love to sing
Sweet sassafras of thee.

The Native Americans of New Hampshire

American Indians had lived in the area that became New Hampshire for thousands of years before Pring's **expedition** arrived. They lived as **nomads,** or people with no established homes. They were hunters who traveled from place to place, wherever they could find food. New Hampshire's plentiful forests and waterways made it an excellent home for the Indians. The forests were filled with deer and bears. The Native Americans hunted these animals using wooden spears with sharp stone tips, and bows and arrows.

New Hampshire's Indian people were powerful and successful hunters. They hunted large animals such as moose, deer, and bears.

Native Americans also fished the streams, lakes, and rivers. These waterways were filled with fish like bass, pike, and trout. For fishing, they used spears, hooks, and nets. Archaeologists (scientists who study past civilizations) have found stone tools and arrowheads buried in the ground throughout New Hampshire.

Then, about 3,000 years ago, the Indians learned to farm. Now, in addition to fishing and hunting, they had another way of getting food. They fashioned gardening tools from wood and clamshells, and fertilized their crops with ground-up fish. The main crops the Native Americans grew were corn (they called corn "maize"), squash, pumpkins, beans, and cucumbers. These crops, along with wild fruits and berries, fish, venison (deer meat), turkeys, and other wild birds, gave New Hampshire's original residents a varied diet.

In addition to hunting, fishing, and farming to feed their own people, the early American Indians traded food and animal skins with other tribes. To reach other tribes, the hunters and traders cut paths through the dense forests. Hundreds of years later, those same paths were used by early European settlers.

Native American Villages

By the time the first European settlers arrived in New Hampshire, most Native Americans were living in villages. These villages were usually located near rivers, lakes, or the ocean, so that fish were readily available. Archaeologists have found evidence of ancient Indian villages along what are called today the Merrimack, Connecticut, Androscoggin, and Saco rivers of New Hampshire.

The forests and waterways of New Hampshire provided Native Americans with everything they needed to survive.

The Native Americans hunted in creative ways. "Deer drives" were fences made from wooden posts. These fences were up to 2 miles (3.2 kilometers) long, built in the shape of a "V." Hunters at the wide opening at the top of the "V" drove the deer down toward its narrow point. There, other hunters waited with bows and arrows, and spears. Trapped by the fences, the deer were easy targets.

Native hunters also kept fields of tall grass to lure deer out of the safety of the forest and into the open (the deer liked eating grass). There, they were easy to kill. Ground traps were also set to snare deer, bears, rabbits, raccoons, moose, and wild birds like turkeys, pigeons, quails, and geese.

While the main purpose of hunting and trapping was to acquire meat for food, no part of the animal went to waste. Skins and furs were used for clothing and to build homes. Stiff hair from the animals' tails was used for **embroidery** and decorations. Tools and arrowheads were crafted from antlers. Hooves served as rattles in native ceremonies. Bones were turned into hairpins, needles, and handles. Bags and containers were made from bladders. **Tendons** were used as bowstrings. Meat was preserved by cutting it into thin strips, then drying it over smoking fires.

Wigwams

To construct their villages, the Indians began by cutting down trees. To do this, they used a technique called "girdling." A deep cut was made all the way around a tree's trunk. Eventually, the tree died and could be knocked over, then cut up and used as firewood. Once an area was cleared of trees, homes could be built and farming could begin.

The early natives lived in structures called **wigwams**. The frames for these dome-shaped homes were made from tree branches. Animal skins were then attached to the wooden frames to create the outside walls. Between five and ten people lived in each wigwam. Each village had between

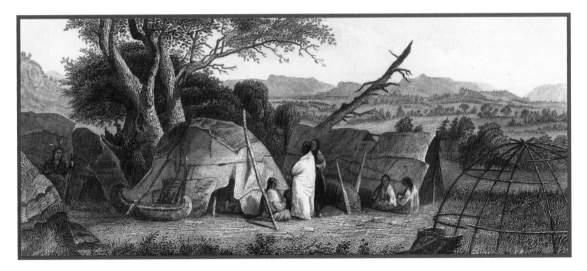

Indians lived in dome-shaped houses called wigwams. Wigwams were very sturdy, but they could be taken apart easily so the Indians could move to a new location.

ten and twenty wigwams. Evidence discovered by archaeologists indicates that between 100 and 200 people lived in a typical New Hampshire Indian village.

The Native Americans of New Hampshire belonged to the Abenaki Indian family. The language they spoke was called Algonquian. The Abenaki Indian family, in turn, was made up of a number of tribes living in different areas of New Hampshire. The Pennacook lived in the Merrimack River valley near what is now the city of Concord. They were the largest and most powerful tribe in the area. The Piscataqua lived in the eastern part of New Hampshire, near what is now Dover. The Nashua made their home in the south, near the city that today bears their name. The Ossipee lived in the northeast, near the Androscoggin River. The Coosuc tribe had villages along the Connecticut River in the northwest. Other tribes included the Squamscott, the Cocheco, and the Pemigewasset.

Family Roles

The men, women, and children of the Abenaki tribes had clearly defined responsibilities. The men did the hunting and fishing. They also built the wigwams and canoes. Some canoes were made by carving out a single log. These were called dugout canoes. Birch bark canoes were made by attaching the bark of birch trees to a wooden frame.

The Indians of New Hampshire built canoes from hollowed-out logs and from the bark of the birch tree.

Women did the farming, planting the crops and tending the fields. They did the cooking, making stews from the vegetables they grew combined with the meat or fish brought back by the men. Tribes that lived near the ocean also ate lobster and clams. Women made maple syrup from tree sap. They created certain dishes, such as succotash—a highly nutritious combination of corn and beans—that were eventually embraced by European colonists.

Children learned skills by watching their parents. They knew that one day they would use these skills as the adult leaders of the tribe. Boys learned to hunt and fish from their fathers. Girls learned to farm and cook from their mothers. All children were taught the spiritual beliefs of the tribe. These beliefs differed greatly from those of the European colonists who would one day arrive in New Hampshire.

Native American Beliefs

Indian life revolved around ancient customs and the changing of the seasons. The Native Americans believed that their world was guided by many spirits—the spirits of the rivers, the land, the mountains, and the forest. All of these spirits were under the guidance of the Great Spirit. Children were taught to offer prayers to these spirits before entering their domain. A prayer to the river spirit was said to ensure a safe crossing. A prayer to the spirit of the forest was offered before entering the woods.

Life for the Indians of precolonial New Hampshire was not easy, but the land gave them what they needed to survive. It offered game, fish, crops, and fresh water. The trees and animals gave them clothing, fire, and materials to build tools, boats, and homes. The Native Americans looked at the land as a gift from the Great Spirit. Land was not something that people could own as personal property. The land was there for the people to use and take care of, and in return it offered them everything they needed. They saw no reason to ever change their way of life.

The Abenaki view of the land they lived on was very different from the view of the Europeans, who were soon to arrive in great numbers. The Europeans saw the "New World" of North America as a tremendous source of natural resources there for the taking. They also believed that land could be owned by governments and individuals.

These two very different points of view came into conflict as the settlers who would build the New Hampshire colony began arriving on the shores of America. In the early 1600s, there were between 3,000 and 5,000 Abenaki Indians living there. Little about their way of life had changed in thousands of years. The arrival of the Europeans and the establishment of the New Hampshire Colony would transform the Native Americans' way of life in less than a century.

Following the Seasons

The Abenaki of New Hampshire were busy throughout all four seasons. In spring, sap ran from birch and maple trees. The Indians made the sap into maple syrup, sugar, and candy. The ground grew soft enough to **till** so crops could be planted. Throughout the summer, the Indians tended the crops; fishing was plentiful. Fall brought the crop harvest, the cutting and storing of firewood, and preparations for the winter hunt. The Abenaki used snowshoes and toboggans to travel through the deep snows of winter, when they set traps and hunted game.

The Algonquian Language

Although the Abenaki had no written language, many words from their spoken language, Algonquian, are still with us today.

Words such as *squaw*, *papoose*, *succotash*, and *tomahawk* are familiar to most people. Here are a few words used by the Abenaki:

acadia = the earth
algonquian = people of the other shore
appalachian = people of the other side
apponaug = oyster
casco = muddy
cochituate = swift river
cummaquid = harbor
hoosac = mountain rock
meriden = pleasant valley
misquamicut = well-wooded country

Exploration Before Martin Pring

Although Martin Pring was the first European to land in and explore New Hampshire, historians believe that the first sailors to see its shores were from Norway. They may have arrived there in the eleventh century. Since there was no written history at that time, it is unknown whether these Europeans ever even saw the Abenaki.

Late in the fifteenth century, an Italian sailor named Giovanni Caboto, who was called John Cabot by the English, also saw the land that would become New Hampshire. Cabot sailed along the Atlantic coast past New Hampshire, all the way down to Virginia. He returned to England with reports of a lush coastline filled with thick forests and flowing rivers.

Cabot was followed in 1524 by an Italian explorer named Giovanni da Verrazano. Verrazano went home with similar tales of great natural riches. He told of animals whose fur was valuable in Europe and of vast amounts of fish in the coastal waters. He also told of sassafras trees, the roots of which were used as medicine in Europe.

Word spread through Europe about a New World filled with resources ripe for the taking. By the late 1500s, fishing ships from several European nations had crossed the Atlantic to fish the waters along the eastern coast of North America.

These early Europeans seemed to have no interest in establishing permanent homes or farming the new land. They were content to take home huge quantities of fish. They also brought goods from Europe, which they traded for furs with the Abenaki. Items such as metal hooks for fishing, iron kettles for cooking, knives, and other metal tools were exchanged for animal furs. The animal furs were used to make hats, coats, and other luxury items in Europe.

The Abenaki were probably amazed when the first Europeans sailed into view. They had never seen anything like these ships with tall wooden **masts** and great billowing sails. The Abenaki called the ships "walking islands," because the masts looked like trees, the sails like clouds, and the ships themselves like islands moving under their own power across the water.

Compared to the Indians' canoes, European ships seemed like floating islands.

More European Exploration

In 1605, two years after Martin Pring's visit, French explorer Samuel de Champlain sailed to New Hampshire. He traveled inland along the Merrimack River, where he met the Abenaki. Champlain gave the natives European goods as gifts.

Exploring the land, he found nut trees, grapevines, and crops planted by the Indians. Champlain wrote in his journal that the people he encountered "cultivated the land and sowed seeds." He also described a large lake, most likely Lake Winnipesaukee, and the distant peaks of what might have been the White Mountains.

Like Pring before him, Champlain, a true explorer at heart, returned home to report his discoveries. He was not interested in settling in this beautiful but wild and harsh land. He wanted only to explore undiscovered parts of the world.

Nine years later, Captain John Smith of England arrived in New Hampshire. Smith had already established the first permanent English colony in the New World, at Jamestown, Virginia, in 1607. Starting in 1614, John Smith would begin building a colony on New Hampshire's shores.

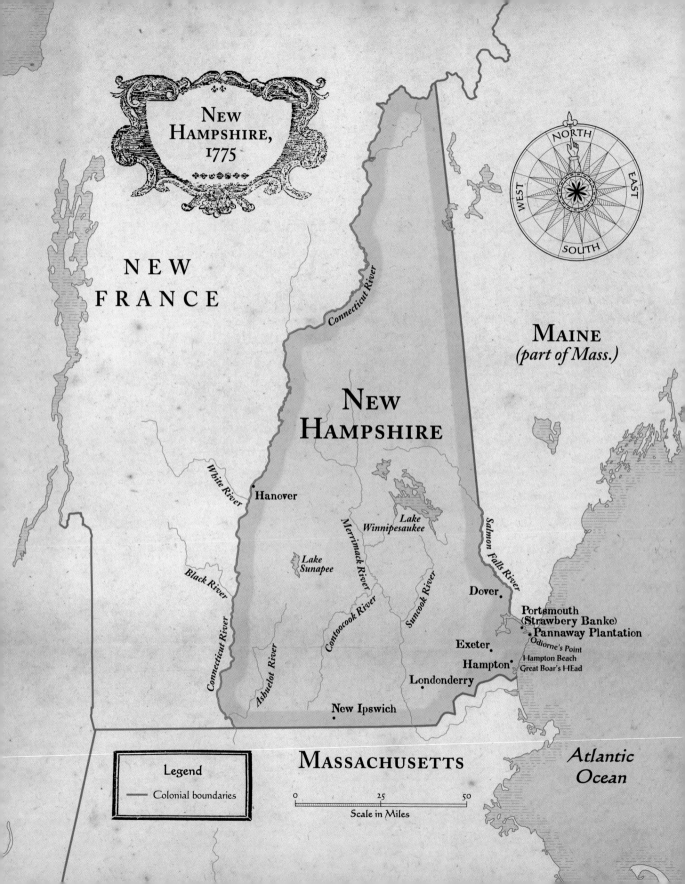

NEW
HAMPSHIRE,
1775

NEW
FRANCE

NORTH

WEST   EAST

SOUTH

MAINE
(part of Mass.)

Connecticut River

NEW
HAMPSHIRE

White River

• Hanover

*Lake
Winnipesaukee*

Merrimack River

*Lake
Sunapee*

Salmon Falls River

Black River

Dover •

Portsmouth
(Strawbery Banke)
• Pannaway Plantation

Contoocook River

Suncook River

• Odiorne's Point
Hampton Beach
Great Boar's HEad

Exeter •

Connecticut River

Ashuelot River

Hampton •

Londonderry •

New Ipswich
•

MASSACHUSETTS

*Atlantic
Ocean*

Legend

—— Colonial boundaries

0   25   50

Scale in Miles

CHAPTER TWO
First Settlements

****

Captain John Smith strongly supported building colonies in the New World. He believed in the independent spirit of people who were willing to take chances by starting new lives in unexplored places. He believed in freedom, independence, and hard work. These beliefs had helped him establish the Jamestown colony in Virginia. They also led him to encourage other people back home in England to make their way to the New World, get land, and start new lives.

In 1609, while living in the Jamestown colony, Smith was severely injured in an explosion. He was forced to return to England. Once he had recovered, Smith longed to return to the New World. In 1614, he got his chance. He led an expedition back to America, to capture whales, find gold, and bring fish and furs back for sale in England.

Smith never caught a whale. He did not discover any gold. But the expedition did serve several useful purposes.

This map is of New Hampshire in 1775.

19

Traveling the coasts of what is now Maine, New Hampshire, Massachusetts, and Rhode Island, Smith created the first detailed maps of the area. He also took notes about the land, the native people, and the plants and animals there. John Smith named this region of North America "New England," a name that still applies today.

Smith's Description of New England

In 1616, Smith wrote a book about his journey called *A Description of New England*. One thing he reported was that he and his crew caught and brought back to England 60,000 fish during their month-long expedition. People in England realized that fishing in North America was a good way to make money. Fishing would become a main part of New Hampshire's economy.

Smith also wrote that this New World was just the place for English settlers searching for freedom and independence. "Here should be no landlords to rack us with high rents," he wrote. "Here every man may be master of his own labor and land in a short time. If a man work but three days in seven, he may get more than he can spend."

Smith's words excited many people to the possibilities of a new life and riches in the land across the sea. Interest in starting a new colony ran high. England's king, James I, realized that people were interested in going to the New World.

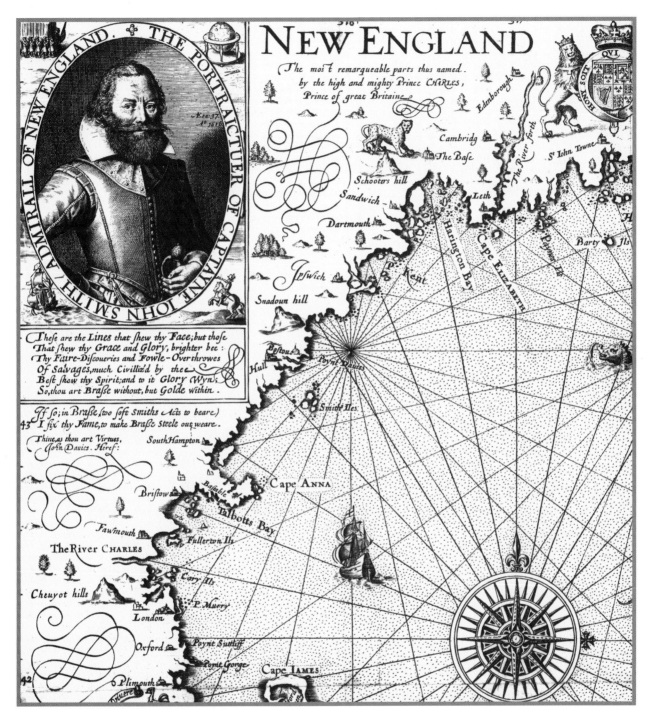

This map, showing the territory John Smith called New England, was published in 1620.

The Council for New England

In 1620, the king formed an organization called the Council for New England. This council was made up of forty business leaders. It gave land **grants** to people who wanted to colonize New England. A land grant was a document that stated that a person owned a piece of land.

The king and the council believed that they had the right to give out ownership of land in North America. The council members hoped that those who accepted these grants would settle and work the land. They also hoped that in return for the grants the settlers would send back to England some of the riches the new land had to offer.

Jeremy Belknap, New Hampshire's first historian, wrote in his book *The History of New Hampshire* in the late eighteenth century, "the Council for New England was the foundation [in charge] of all the land grants that were made of the country of New-England." However, this group of English business leaders had simply decided to divide up land they had never seen.

The land had never been explored or mapped by Europeans. In time, as more and more settlers made their way to New Hampshire, more than one person would claim to own the same piece of land. This led to many fights and other problems in the years to come.

In 1622, two members of the council, John Mason and Ferdinando Gorges, were given a huge land grant. That meant that they could send people to New England to settle the land. The owners would earn money from the sale of furs and crops sent back home by the settlers.

The Mayflower

In 1620, the Council for New England gave a land grant to a group of settlers who called themselves Pilgrims. They sailed to Plymouth in what is now Massachusetts aboard the ship the *Mayflower* and founded England's second permanent settlement.

John Mason was a merchant and an officer in the English navy. He had been governor of the English settlement in Newfoundland in Canada from 1615 to 1621. His strong belief in the importance of colonization led him to join the Council for New England in 1621.

Sir Ferdinando Gorges was an English soldier and the son of a wealthy landowner. For years he had heard tales from returning explorers of the riches to be found in the New World. Upon reading Captain John Smith's book *A Description of New England*, Gorges decided he wanted to start a new colony. In 1620, he was named the first president of the newly formed Council for New England.

The joint grant given to Mason and Gorges covered the land from the Kennebec River in what would become Maine to the Merrimack River in what would soon be called New

Hampshire. According to Jeremy Belknap in *The History of New Hampshire*, the land given to these two men and bordered by two rivers also "extended back to the great lakes and rivers of Canada." It was a huge stretch of uncharted forest that would eventually become several states.

The first settlers in New Hampshire landed at Odiorne's Point in 1623.

Pannaway Plantation

Although Mason and Gorges were the first to receive a land grant in New Hampshire, they were not the first to establish a settlement. In 1623, the council granted 6,000 acres (2,400 hectares) to an English pharmacist named David Thomson. He planned to start a plantation (a large farm) on the Piscataqua River in New Hampshire. He hoped to grow crops, mine for gold, fish the waters, and trade with the native people. Thompson and about twenty other settlers (all men) landed at Odiorne's Point, near the modern town of Rye.

Thompson named the settlement Pannaway Plantation. *Pannaway* is an Abenaki word meaning "little harbor." He could not have chosen a better location. The plantation had clean, plentiful drinking water, fertile soil, and great fishing. Local Abenaki tribes were friendly to the arriving strangers.

Pannaway Plantation is generally considered the first permanent English settlement in New Hampshire. The settlers lived in one main building and put up another, smaller building where they traded European goods with the Abenaki. The plantation also had workshops, including a blacksmith's shop. The blacksmith put shoes on the horses and made metal tools. The settlers built a number of wooden platforms called "stages." The fish that the men caught would be dried on these stages. Once dried, the fish could make the long journey back to England without spoiling.

Soon, Thomson's wife, Amias, joined him at Pannaway Plantation. Amias Thompson was the first European woman to live in New Hampshire. Several years later, for reasons unknown to historians, David and Amias Thompson left Pannaway Plantation. Without Thomson's leadership, Pannaway Plantation soon began to lose money and all the people left.

Around the same time that David Thompson founded Pannaway Plantation, two brothers, Edward and William Hilton, started their own settlement. It would eventually become the New Hampshire town of Dover, but it was first called Hilton's Point. Pannaway may have preceded Hilton's Point by a few months to claim the title of the first European settlement in New Hampshire, but Pannaway Plantation was gone after a few years, while Dover is today one of New Hampshire's biggest cities.

Relationship Between the Settlers and the Abenaki

When the first English settlers of New Hampshire arrived, they lived in relative peace with the Abenaki. The Indians taught them to grow corn, a crop with which the Europeans were unfamiliar. The Native Americans also taught the settlers how to build canoes and snowshoes and how to tap maple trees for sap to make sugar. The Native Americans openly shared their methods of planting, tanning animal hides (turning the raw hide into usable leather), and trapping. They even taught the newcomers the native game of lacrosse.

This early contact between natives and settlers mainly involved trade. The settlers received fur pelts from the Indians. In return, the English traded many items brought from Europe—cloth, guns and gunpowder, glass, liquor, iron pots, metal fishhooks, axes, and other tools. The Abenaki had never seen any of these things before.

The Three Sisters

The most common crops grown by the colonists were corn, beans, and squash. The three crops were planted together in a specific pattern, learned from the Native Americans, who called this grouping of the plants "the Three Sisters." Beans grow on vine-like stems, which need poles to wrap themselves around. Cornstalks grow tall, providing the perfect pole for the beans to twist around. Squash grows low to the ground and produces large, flat leaves. These leaves protect the bases of all three plants, keeping weeds down and helping the soil to stay moist.

New Hampshire's earliest settlers brought everything they needed to establish a new colony, including livestock such as sheep, cows, and chickens.

But the settlers also brought something else with them, something deadly.

European diseases like smallpox, measles, and scarlet fever were unknown to the Abenaki. They caught these diseases from the settlers. A simple handshake transferred the deadly germs to the unprepared natives. Huge epidemics ripped through the Abenaki tribes. Entire villages were wiped out. In a three-year period, over 75 percent of the Abenaki died from these diseases. Many of the survivors fled, leaving empty villages of the dead behind. This great disaster made it fairly easy for the colonists to take land away from the tribes in the years to come.

Strawbery Banke

In 1629, John Mason and Sir Ferdinando Gorges decided to split the enormous land grant that had been given to them seven years earlier. Gorges kept the land from the Kennebec to the Piscataqua, later naming his land Maine.

Mason took the land that ran from the Piscataqua to the Merrimack. Mason named his territory New Hampshire, in honor of his home county, Hampshire, in England. He wasted no time in sending colonists there. In 1630, Mason sent his first group of settlers to New Hampshire aboard a great ship called the *Warwick*.

Upon arrival in New Hampshire, the ship sailed about 2 miles (3.2 kilometers) up the Piscataqua River, where the new colonists stepped ashore. They found wild strawberries growing along the riverbank as far as they could see. They decided to start their settlement at that spot, which they named Strawbery Banke. This settlement eventually grew into the town of Portsmouth, one of New Hampshire's most important towns.

Like the other New Hampshire colonists, the Strawbery Banke settlers fished, hunted, grew crops, and traded with the native people. Strawbery Banke had a main building, where the settlers lived and traded. It also had a sawmill for creating lumber from the trees of the New Hampshire forests. Lumber would quickly become a major New Hampshire resource.

The community prospered, and within ten years close to two hundred people were living at Strawbery Banke. But John Mason never made it back to the New World himself. He never saw the great settlement that he had started. Mason died in 1635. His heirs inherited his land. They also inherited the many disputes and lawsuits over exact property lines and claims of ownership that would plague the family for more than a century.

Religious Freedom

Life for most settlers who lived in the New England colonies was similar in many ways. Even so, some of the colonies themselves were started for different reasons. Most of the settlers who came to live in New Hampshire, for example, were looking to make money. They hoped to tap into the riches that could be made from the region's fishing, hunting, and timber. But not all of the English colonists came to the New World for commercial reasons.

The Massachusetts Bay Colony, located just south of New Hampshire, was started for a different reason. It was founded in the late 1620s by people who left England desiring religious freedom. These people felt that the Church of England had become dishonest and heavily influenced by Roman Catholics. They wanted to practice a form of Christianity that was simpler, with less ritual. They considered this branch of the religion purer, and so they called themselves Puritans.

By the late 1630s, a group of the Puritans in Massachusetts began speaking out against the Puritan church's practices. The group was led by a minister named John Wheelwright. Wheelwright and his followers were banished from the colony by the Puritan church because they had spoken out against it. They moved north into New Hampshire. In 1638, they founded the town of Exeter. There, they could practice their religion, since New Hampshire **imposed** no religious rules.

A year later, a minister named Stephen Batchelor and his followers left Massachusetts and started the town of Hampton, in New Hampshire. They, too, were searching for more religious freedom. By 1640, four strong towns had been established in New Hampshire: Dover, Strawbery Banke (which would become Portsmouth), Exeter, and Hampton.

Massachusetts Control

The following year, these four towns and all of New Hampshire came under the control of Massachusetts. Each town was able to make its own rules about religion. Each town also sent a person to represent it at the General Court in Boston. This court discussed issues that were important to the entire colony. New Hampshire remained a part of Massachusetts for the next thirty-eight years.

Because New Hampshire was now considered part of Massachusetts, people from Massachusetts were free to move north into the New Hampshire region. This led to economic growth in New Hampshire. Farms, lumber mills, and grain mills sprang up in the previously unexplored western areas of New Hampshire.

Grain Mills

Grain mills were used to grind crops like wheat or rye into fine, powdery flour. Beans and seeds were also ground into flour. The flour was then used in cooking and baking. Corn was also ground into cornmeal, a useful cooking ingredient. Most mills were built above moving water. The water ran through the lowest level of the mill, turning a waterwheel. The waterwheel then turned a rough milling stone that crushed the grain, turning it into flour.

It was not only economic opportunity that attracted people from Massachusetts to New Hampshire. New Hampshire also offered greater religious freedoms than were available in strictly Puritan Massachusetts. Quakers, for example, had been persecuted in Massachusetts for having different beliefs than the Puritans. Many fled the colony for the tolerant ways of New Hampshire.

Conflict with the Abenaki

The growth of New Hampshire would eventually lead to warfare between the settlers and the Abenaki. Native Americans and English settlers had lived mostly in peace for almost fifty years. The natural riches that New Hampshire offered appeared to be enough to satisfy everyone. But as the number of settlers grew, the Abenaki villages were threatened. Natives and settlers began competing for the natural resources.

The late 1600s was a time of brutal war between settlers and natives in New Hampshire and throughout all of New England. When the first settlers had arrived in the early 1600s, more than 10,000 Abenaki lived in the area that was to become New Hampshire. By 1700, fewer than 1,200 remained.

CHAPTER THREE

Daily Life

****

Tough-Minded Colonists

Residents of New Hampshire have always had a reputation for being tough-minded, hardworking, independent people. This well-earned reputation was forged during the colonial days. New arrivals from England faced a land with a cold climate and a short growing season, rocky soil, and long, harsh winters. But the New Hampshire colonists, in many ways, turned these hardships to their advantage, using what they found to carve out new lives. Despite difficult conditions, they survived, even thrived.

The vast forests of New Hampshire provided wood to build homes. The settlers chopped down trees and used the wood to build the outside walls. In his 1899 book *Colonial Life in New Hampshire*, New Hampshire historian J. H. Fassett describes the rest of the house-building process:

The kitchen was the center of the home for New Hampshire settlers. The fireplace held a large pot for cooking and for heating water to wash clothes.

The well-trodden earth served as a floor, and the roof was of saplings covered with birch-bark. The chinks between the logs were packed with moss and clay, so that not even the coldest wind could beat through them.

The heart of a colonial house was its fireplace and chimney. These were built with bricks, which were made, according to Fassett, of "rough stones laid in clay." The fireplace provided warmth to heat the home and flame for cooking and baking. A fire was lit by striking a piece of steel against a rough flint stone. This created a spark, which ignited a piece of cloth. The cloth then lit the wood.

Because it was such a difficult task to start a fire, families hoped that some glowing embers of the fire from the day before would still remain the next morning. Then new wood could be added to ignite large, warming flames. If the embers were cold, however, the boys in the family had to walk to a neighbor's farm to borrow some fire to relight their hearth. This could be a journey of several miles through the cold New Hampshire woods.

Besides the light from the fire, colonists used oil lamps to light their homes. The oil was often taken from the bodies of codfish or whales, which the colonists hunted, and placed into glass lamps with cloth wicks. The wick absorbed the oil, which burned for many hours.

Most colonial families did not own clocks, which were considered a luxury, afforded only by the wealthy. Most colonial families used hourglasses and sundials, or relied on bells in the town's meetinghouse or church to toll out the hour.

Several dishes learned from the Abenaki became staples of the colonists' menu. Succotash, made from corn and beans, was a regular part of their diet. So were cornmeal, corn bread, and porridge. Squares of porridge could be frozen (in snow) and taken by the men as a **portable** breakfast when they left on hunting expeditions.

In the spring, when the sap was running in the maple trees, the colonists made maple syrup, maple sugar, and maple candy. They learned how to do this from the Abenaki. Using an axe, the men cut through the bark of maple trees. They then placed wooden troughs (like buckets) beneath the cuts to capture the dripping sap. When enough sap was collected, it was put into a large kettle over a fire and boiled. Thick syrup resulted. The syrup could also be made into maple candy.

Maple Candy

Maple syrup was spread thinly in shallow pans, which were then placed out in the snow. The cold from the snow hardened the syrup into a brittle sheet, which was broken into pieces of delicious, sweet candy. Colonial children greatly looked forward each spring to gobbling down their maple candy.

The Forests of New Hampshire

While most families used wood from the forests to build and then heat their homes, some colonists grew wealthy by harvesting the trees for lumber. Sawmills popped up all over New Hampshire. Trees were milled into lumber, which could be shipped back to England. Eventually, shipbuilding became a profitable trade for many colonists. The large supply of wood, the nearby sawmills, and miles of coastline provided the perfect combination for building ships.

The most prized trees in the New Hampshire forests were white pines, which grew to heights of 200 feet (60 meters). Their straight, strong timbers were greatly sought after by the British navy. White pines were the finest trees available for making masts for warships. The tallest and strongest white pines were marked with arrow symbols cut with an ax. Any tree marked with the "King's Broad Arrow," as the symbol was known, immediately became the king's property. Anyone who cut these trees down faced heavy fines. Special ships were built to haul these extremely heavy trees back to England.

Farm Life

Most settlers did not get rich from the timber of the New Hampshire forests. Most were farmers, who had to clear stones from the rocky soil before they could plant their crops. As the stones were removed from the ground, they were stacked up to create stone walls. These walls often marked property boundaries. Many of these walls still stand today as reminders of the hardiness and creativity of the colonists.

Farmers had to clear large rocks and stumps from their fields before they could plant crops.

Daily colonial life was filled with the many chores necessary to house, feed, and clothe the family. These tasks were strictly split up among the men, women, boys, and girls of each family. Men prepared the soil for planting, planted the crops, hunted, fished, and chopped wood. They also sheared sheep for wool. Women cooked, cleaned, and made clothes, spinning wool and flax on spinning wheels. They also made soap and candles, took care of the children, and tended the garden once the crops were planted. Boys and girls milked cows and did other farm chores. Mostly they worked with their parents, learning the skills they would use one day when they had families of their own.

Boys and girls in colonial New Hampshire helped with the farm work. This girl is bringing the cows back to the barn for milking.

Colonial farmers faced many hardships. For example, they were at the mercy of the weather. An entire summer's worth of backbreaking labor in the field could be wiped out by a single hailstorm. Floods, drought, and early frosts, as well as insects, mice, and rats, could destroy crops that had been carefully tended for months. If the fall harvest was less than expected, a farmer faced the problem of not having enough hay or grain to feed the livestock through the harsh New Hampshire winter.

Cows, oxen, and other livestock were an important part of farm life. Among other things, they provided food and milk, and pulled plows and wagons for the farmers. Colonial farmers raised animals descended from those brought over from England.

Nature's Pests

The farmers of the New Hampshire colony constantly battled pests of all kinds. Worms, flies, and caterpillars devoured entire fields of barley, corn, and wheat. Wolves, wildcats, and bears threatened crops and livestock.

Raccoons seemed to wait until a week before the corn crop was ripe, then creep in at night, ruining the harvest. Passenger pigeons migrated through the colony in early fall, just as the corn was ready. Called "maize thieves," a large flock could destroy a whole field of corn in minutes.

New Hampshire Tradesmen

Besides farmers, the New Hampshire colony included artisans and **tradesmen** whose businesses helped the colony grow and prosper. Tanning, for example, became a useful and profitable trade. A tanner took a cow's or horse's hide and first cleaned it of dirt and remaining pieces of the animal's flesh. The hide was then soaked in a vat of tanning solution—water mixed with ground-up tree bark—which loosened the hair. The final step was to scrape off the hair.

The tanned leather was made into boots, shoes, aprons, and other types of clothing. It was also used for saddles and to bind books. Tanneries were usually located near a pond, brook, or river, because tanning required a large supply of water for soaking and cleaning the animal hides.

Most tradesmen, like carpenters, blacksmiths, shoemakers, wig makers, tanners, and shipbuilders, were organized into guilds, similar to today's labor unions. If a farmer's son wanted to learn a trade, he served an apprenticeship. This training period usually lasted for seven years.

During his apprenticeship, a boy was practically owned by his teacher. He worked very hard in exchange for room and board, clothing, and, of course, the learning of a valuable skill. For example, a shoemaker's apprentice would start by learning to measure a customer's feet. He would then gain experience by choosing a wooden model of the type of shoe that the customer needed. The shoemaker would then use the measurements and the model to craft the shoe. By working with the shoemaker in this way, the apprentice would eventually learn the entire process of shoemaking himself.

Horseshoes were made by the blacksmith who nailed them to a horse's hooves. He also made most of the metal objects used by the settlers.

Traveling Tradesmen

Some colonists made their living as traveling tradesmen, going from house to house offering their services. Some carried ladle and spoon molds to make new silverware. They melted old, damaged, or worn-out spoons over fire, pouring the liquid metal into the molds. When the metal cooled and hardened, brand-new spoons popped out of the molds.

Shoemakers also traveled from house to house. They made shoes for the whole family, using leather provided by the household. The leather was taken from the tanned skins of the farmer's own cattle.

As new settlements sprang up, the call went out for skilled craftsmen to move to the new towns. A new settlement that boasted a blacksmith or tanner could more easily attract other colonists.

The Doctors of Old New Hampshire

The village doctor was very important in New Hampshire. He was just as important as the schoolmaster or the innkeeper, and almost as respected as the minister. He was welcomed by every family, from the richest to the poorest.

Doctors in the 1700s did not have much education. Most of them served only a short apprenticeship with a physician, either in Europe or in a large colonial city. There were no medical colleges in the colonies until late in the century. The practice of bloodletting for almost any disease was common. In bloodletting, a certain amount of blood was drained from the body in an effort to rid the body of illness. If the physician was not available, bloodletting might be done by the barber or the minister. Drugs were few, and not much was known about their proper use. Herbs were used, such as valerian for pain, St. John's wort for melancholy (sadness), and coltsfoot for coughs.

Colonial Folk Remedy

Doctors were scarce in the New Hampshire colony, so many colonists turned to homemade folk remedies such as this one for toothaches and swelling of the jaw:

Boil a gruel (a thin porridge) made of flour, maize, and milk; to this add some fat of hogs and stir well so that everything mixes equally. Soak a handkerchief in this mixture, while it is still hot, then place it on the swollen area. Leave it there until it cools down.

Time for Fun

The colonists developed creative ways to have fun even when they were working hard. Chores such as corn-husking, or removing the husks from ears of corn so that the corn could be eaten, were done in a large group. These "husking bees" were a chance to socialize with neighbors.

Women held quilting bees, during which they produced warm blankets while exchanging local news. "Raisings," the putting up of buildings (such as barns, meetinghouses, or homes) brought together entire communities. They turned the serious work of building into an entertaining group activity.

At county fairs, the colonists enjoyed sports and contests. Wrestling was popular among the men, as were other competitions, such as races to see who was the fastest runner. Other contests were held to judge whose apples were the reddest, whose oxen could drag a stone the farthest, whose horse ran the fastest, or whose homemade jam was the tastiest.

Children in the New Hampshire Colony

Although most children worked hard at their chores on the family farm, they also found time for fun and games. Many of the games that colonial children played have survived to this day. Colonial children played games such as tag, top spinning, ball games, marbles, and jacks. A game called "scotch hoppers" became hopscotch. "Pickadill" was a game of tag played in the snow. "Poison" was another type of tag in which players hopped from stone to stone. If they stepped off the stones, they were tagged out, or "poisoned."

Children also played leapfrog, vaulting over each other's backs. Children in the New Hampshire colony enjoyed blowing bubbles. They used soapy water, although they did not have today's plastic wand to help. They simply spread their soapy fingers and blew. Children flew kites made of wood, cloth, and string. Some well-off girls had dolls imported from England, though such toys were rare. In the winter, children skated on frozen lakes and streams.

In addition to doing chores and playing, children in the New Hampshire colony attended school. Reading, writing, simple math, and Bible lessons made up most of what they learned. In 1690, the *New England Primer* was published, becoming the first textbook to be used in the colonies. It contained simple rhymes and pictures to help children learn the alphabet.

A Primer Lesson

Many lessons in the *New England Primer* included religious themes. These rhymes taught both the alphabet and a religious lesson at the same time.

A: In Adam's fall we sinned all.

B: Thy life to mend,
    God's book attend.

J: Job feels the rod,
    yet blesses God.

L: The Lion bold,
    the Lamb doth hold.

Schools had only one room in which children of all ages learned to read, write, and do arithmetic.

Girls almost never received education beyond the basics of reading, writing, and math. Some boys from wealthy families, however, were taught the Greek and Latin languages. Some went to Harvard, the first college in colonial New England. Founded in 1636, Harvard is still in Cambridge, Massachusetts. New Hampshire's first college, Dartmouth, would not open until 1769.

When the children of wealthy colonists got married, their parents provided them with a number of things necessary to begin their new lives. Sons got land to start their own farms. Daughters got household items such as bed linens, mirrors, cooking kettles and platters, milk pails, and butter **churns.** Sometimes daughters received a cow as well. These gifts were known as a daughter's "bridal portion."

Children's Clothing

The following is a list of required clothing taken by a well-to-do ten-year-old New Hampshire boy to a boarding school in Massachusetts in the late 1600s:

- 11 new shirts
- 4 pair laced sleeves
- 8 plain cravats (scarves)
- 4 cravats with lace
- 4 striped waistcoats with buttons (a waistcoat is similar to a vest)
- 1 flowered waistcoat
- 1 gray hat with a black ribbon
- 1 gray hat with a blue ribbon
- 1 dozen black buttons
- 3 pair gold buttons
- 3 pair silver buttons
- 2 pair fine blue stockings
- 1 pair fine red stockings
- 4 white handkerchiefs
- 2 speckled handkerchiefs
- 5 pair gloves
- 1 cloth coat
- 1 pair blue plush britches (pants)
- 1 pair serge (wool) britches (pants)
- 2 combs
- 1 pair new shoes
- silk and thread to mend clothes

The Church in the New Hampshire Colony

On Sunday, all work, play, chores, and schooling stopped. Families gathered in each town's central meetinghouse. The minister gave sermons and led the people in prayer. A New Hampshire reverend named David Sutherland described the scene at a typical meetinghouse on a Sunday:

People who owned horses rode them. Those who had them not went on foot. More than one half of the church-going people went on foot. Sleighs or sleds were used in winter. For years we had no stoves in the meeting-house of Bath [his hometown]; and yet in the coldest weather, the house was always full.

The meetinghouse was by far the most important public building in each town. It was used for social gatherings or for town meetings. At these meetings, the men of the town could vote on important issues, such as taxes, and road building construction. Women did not attend town meetings. They had no say in the laws of their towns.

Laws were also passed to govern behavior. Some laws, such as those against murder and theft, still exist today. Other laws showed the role religion played in colonists' lives. It was against the law to work or drink alcohol on Sunday, the Christian Sabbath. Public drunkenness was punished by placing the offender into the stocks, a wooden device that secured a person's head, hands, and feet. Passersby made fun of those in the public stocks.

Guided by a strong pioneering spirit, the colonists of New Hampshire led a simple, if difficult, life. Hard work, strong religious beliefs, clearly defined roles, and strong family ties led to a sense of community.

Slavery in the New Hampshire Colony

Not all people in the New Hampshire colony had the same experience. African-American slaves living there did not have the freedoms that the settlers enjoyed.

The slave trade began in Portsmouth in the mid-1600s. New Hampshire was never home to a large number of slaves. In 1708, there were 70 slaves living in the colony. By the time of the American Revolution in 1776, the slave population had increased to about 650. At that same time, there were over 100,000 slaves living in the Virginia colony.

Slaves in New Hampshire were assigned to many different roles. Wealthy people used slaves as household servants who did daily chores. Slaves were a status symbol for the rich, who could show how rich they were by the number of slaves they owned.

For artisans, merchants, shipowners, and farmers, enslaved men served as skilled craftsmen, heavy laborers on the waterfront, seamen, and farmworkers. Female slaves worked as household servants. They also did gardening and other outdoor work typically performed by women in the colony. The difference was that other women did this work on land owned by their families. All slaves worked only for their masters and could not own any land.

Schools in New Hampshire

Despite the economic and religious advantages that attracted settlers to New Hampshire, the four towns of New Hampshire had never established formal schools. In 1647, Massachusetts passed a law requiring every town in the colony (which included the New Hampshire settlements) of fifty or more people to hire a teacher. The teacher would be paid, at least in part, by taxes collected by the Massachusetts government. This law marked the beginning of the public school system in the United States.

Children's Books

In addition to the formal primers that children read in school, children in the New Hampshire colony also read storybooks and picture books. *Aesop's Fables* was available in a cheaply printed edition. Although not specifically written for children, *Robinson Crusoe*, published in 1714, and *Gulliver's Travels*, published in 1726, were both popular among young people. A small, pocket-sized version of *Jack the Giant Killer*, otherwise known as *Jack and the Beanstalk*, was published in 1744. Books of riddles, called "guess books," were also popular among the children of the New Hampshire colony. In 1760, a book of nursery rhymes was published under the name *Mother Goose's Melodies*. It has remained popular in various forms to this day.

CHAPTER FOUR

Times of Turmoil

✳✳✳✳✳✳✳✳✳✳✳✳✳✳✳✳✳✳✳✳✳✳✳✳✳✳✳✳✳✳✳✳✳✳✳

In 1679, King Charles II decided that New Hampshire should be broken away from Massachusetts's rule and become a royal colony itself. In early 1680, the king appointed John Cutt, a wealthy, prominent citizen of New Hampshire, to be royal governor of the newly formed New Hampshire Colony. The king also named a ruling body called the Governor's Council to help Cutt deal with important issues that affected the entire colony. The small collection of New Hampshire towns, which had been protected by Massachusetts for nearly forty years, was finally a separate, unified colony. But the final word in all important matters in New Hampshire still came from England.

The colony was plunged into turmoil when John Cutt died unexpectedly in March 1681. He was replaced by Richard Waldron as New Hampshire's royal governor. Waldron's dislike of the Abenaki. made the relationship between the natives and the settlers even worse than it was.

☙ *This family prepares for an attack by the Abenaki.*

Because the Abenaki did not think of land as something that could be owned, they did not understand that they were no longer allowed to use their traditional lands, which were now held by the English. To make matters worse, the Abenaki could not read English. They did not realize that they were giving away the rights to the land they had always lived on. It was only when they were not allowed to hunt, trap, fish, and farm on this land that the true intent of the settlers became clear. The Abenaki were angry that they could not enjoy the land of their ancestors. They turned fiercely against the colonists.

King Philip's War

In 1675, the first organized rebellion by the Native Americans against the settlers began. It was led by a **sachem** (the Algonquian word for "chief") named Philip. Small parties of Native Americans raided English settlements. Their attacks were terrifying and destructive. Houses were burned. Men, women, and children were killed or taken captive. This conflict came to be known as King Philip's War.

The Pequot sachem named Metacomet was called King Philip by the English.

King Philip's War brought a huge change to the peaceful lives of the New Hampshire colonists. Fear of Indian raids caused these colonists to set up a **militia**, or local army. Jeremy Belknap describes the shift in the day-to-day lives of the colonists in his *History of New Hampshire*:

The plantations at Portsmouth and Dover were now filled with fear and confusion. Business was suspended, and every man was obliged to provide for his own and his family's safety. Thus the labor of the field was exchanged for the duty of the garrison [fort], and they who had long lived in peace and security were upon their guard night and day, subject to continual alarms and the most fearful apprehensions.

King Philip's War marked the beginning of almost ninety years of war between settlers and natives.

War with the French

The New Hampshire colonists soon got caught up in a conflict between England and its longtime European enemy, France. The roots of this conflict went back to the sixteenth and seventeenth centuries. During those years, England was colonizing the area of North America that would become the eastern United States. Meanwhile, France was busy colonizing the coastline to the north, in the area that would become Canada.

By the late 1600s, France and England each wanted the land that had been claimed by the other. They both sought total control of the New World. But the two countries were interested in controlling North America for different reasons. The English colonized the land with permanent settlements, which grew into towns and cities. The French wanted control of the land so they could trade with the Native Americans. They traded for furs to sell back home in France.

Therefore, when war between the English and the French broke out in the colonies in 1689, most Native Americans sided with the French. The natives and the French got along well. The fur trade helped each party.

The French gave the Native Americans weapons and convinced them to fight with them against the English, who had come to take their land away. For the next seventy-four years, the French and their Indian allies devastated the colonies. War and the fear of war made day-to-day life in New Hampshire harder than it had been before.

☞ *The Huron and other Indian tribes fought on the side of the French against the English colonies.*

There were four major conflicts in which the French and Indians fought against the English. They were King William's War (1689–1697), Queen Anne's War (1702–1713), King George's War (1744–1748), and the French and Indian War (1754–1763).

New Hampshire suffered greatly when the first war started in 1689. Native American raiding parties, armed by the French, attacked swiftly and fiercely. Settlers were killed, scalped, or taken prisoner. When a settler was scalped, the hair and scalp on his or her head was sliced off with a sharp blade. Some Indians collected scalps as proof of their bravery in war. These raids kept the settlers fearful and anxious.

Garrisons

Colonists were afraid to establish new settlements that would be easy targets for Indian attacks. Instead, the colonists made their existing towns stronger and safer. Each village built forts called garrison houses. Everyone in the village helped to build these secure structures and then went to the garrison house each night to sleep in safety. Sentries (guards) were posted at the garrisons, so that someone was always watching for attacks throughout the night while the others slept.

Queen Anne's War

During Queen Anne's War (1702–1713), the French and their Native American allies took as many prisoners as possible. These prisoners were forced to work in French settlements in Canada. Wealthy prisoners were held for high ransoms. The French received payment and goods in exchange for their release.

Prisoners taken from the New Hampshire colonies were forced to travel to Canada by foot. The journey was long and difficult. Historian Jeremy Belknap describes what the colonists faced. He wrote of the "hardships of traveling half naked and barefoot through pathless deserts [deserted places], over craggy mountains and deep swamps, exposed by day and night to the [harsh]…winter weather, and in the summer to the [poisonous] stings of those numberless insects." Children who could not make the long trek were often killed along the way, right in front of their parents.

The colonists fought back. They were just as cruel as the French and the Indians. Abenaki villages were burned to the ground, and their people were slaughtered. The colonists even took to scalping their victims. Colonial governments offered rewards for the scalps of Native Americans, both adults and children.

Help from Massachusetts

The economic cost of war hurt the colonies as well. Fighting against the French and Indians was costly for England. To raise money, the British king increased the taxes that the colonists had to pay. This pattern of raising taxes on the colonists would continue over the next century. It was a constant source of anger for those struggling to create a new life in America.

New Hampshire's colonists formed their own armies called militias. They left their homes to fight when their towns or farms were attacked by French and Indian forces.

When the wars against the French and Indians began, the colonists of New Hampshire felt unable to organize a proper defense. Small local militias had formed during King Philip's War. But they were no match for the well-trained armies of the French and Indians. More and more the colonists believed that their best hope to defend themselves would be to rejoin Massachusetts. That colony was larger, and its army had better equipment.

In 1690, a group of Portsmouth's leading citizens drew up a petition for New Hampshire to once again be part of Massachusetts. They collected more than 350 signatures of colonists who agreed with them. The petition was presented to the governor, the Governor's Council, and the General Court of Massachusetts. They all quickly accepted the proposal. A lieutenant governor would rule over New Hampshire and report to the governor of Massachusetts. This arrangement would remain in effect until 1741.

The average person in colonial America probably had very little clothing. One would have been very lucky to own two full changes of clothing for everyday use and one outfit for Sunday or special occasions.

❦ Bonnets such as these were part of every female wardrobe—young and old, rich and poor.

✑ Fine clothes like this man's coat and fancy woman's dress were rare. The fabric was expensive. Each garment took hours to make by hand. Only wealthy colonists could afford them.

☞ ☞ Simpler clothes were worn for everyday chores like cooking and farming.

Clothing

⌐ Simple clothing, an apron, and a hat was the usual outfit for a field slave.

◁ Top coat, waistcoat, frilly blouse, breeches, stockings, and silver-buckled leather shoes showed a person was wealthy.

☞ Commonly made from wool felt, the three-cornered hat was the typical headgear of colonial America.

▷ Close-fitting breeches and stockings were more popular than long pants.

⚓ Skill was required to craft wigs, which men and women of the upper class wore every day.

CHAPTER FIVE

A Growing Colony

✳✳✳✳✳✳✳✳✳✳✳✳✳✳✳✳✳✳✳✳✳✳✳✳✳✳✳✳✳✳✳✳✳

Peace for England and France

The constant warfare took its toll on the growth of the New Hampshire colony. By 1690, New Hampshire had almost stopped growing. Many people lost their lives or were captured in Abenaki attacks. Others simply left their homes in New Hampshire for the safer colonies of Massachusetts and Connecticut.

Then, in 1713, England and France signed a peace **treaty**, agreeing to stop fighting. News of this treaty soon reached the colonies. The French settlers and Native Americans agreed to meet with the British colonists in Portsmouth to sign their own peace treaty. This ended Queen Anne's War, which had been raging since 1702.

🖎 *Most of New Hampshire's settlers lived on small farms spread throughout the colony's many wooded valleys.*

A Period of Growth

Peace would last for thirty years, a period of rapid growth in New Hampshire. Young couples settled in the colony and began raising families. Immigration increased in the years after the peace treaty was signed. Increased trade between the colony and England led many young merchants to settle in New Hampshire. Some English sailors and soldiers left the military and found work in the colony. Immigrants also came from the islands of the British West Indies in the Caribbean Sea. There, land had become so expensive that some residents decided to come to the colonies.

New Hampshire also experienced a **migration** of colonists from Massachusetts, Rhode Island, and Connecticut. As children from these other New England colonies grew up, many were eager for land and homes of their own. Land in the colonies in which they were born had become expensive because most of it had already been settled. These young people looked to New Hampshire and its vast supply of land and timber.

The New Hampshire government was anxious for more settlers and encouraged these moves. Land was reasonably priced, and New Hampshire's rivers made travel and moving fairly easy.

The Scotch-Irish

By far the biggest group of immigrants during this time came to New Hampshire from the area of northern Ireland known as Ulster. This was home mostly to people of Scottish descent. In 1719, these "Scotch-Irish," as they were known, began buying land in New Hampshire. They soon founded the town of Londonderry, named for the city in Ireland from which they had come.

Londonderry thrived and grew through the next few decades. The Scotch-Irish had originally left their homeland to escape religious persecution. They were welcomed in New Hampshire as hardworking members of the colony. They brought with them skills and culture that quickly became part of New Hampshire's daily life.

The Scotch-Irish introduced the potato as an important crop in North America. The potato became a valuable part of the colonists' diets. The Scotch-Irish also brought with them the skill of growing flax, from which linen and lace fabrics were made.

The flax plant was the main source of cloth for New Hampshire's settlers.

It took hours of work to spin flax into yarn. Much of the work was done by colonial girls who learned to use a spinning wheel at a young age.

Flax was a difficult crop to grow in New Hampshire. The rocky New Hampshire soil had to be plowed before the flaxseeds could be planted. Plowing was difficult. The man of the household led teams of oxen, which pulled heavy plows. The plow blades churned up the earth. This was done once the ground thawed, usually in April or May. Entire families then walked the freshly plowed fields tossing the flaxseeds in a wide pattern. More than a year would go by between the time that the seeds were planted and the time that the fabrics made from the flax were completed.

Flax was spun into yarn on spinning wheels. The yarn was then woven into fabric on looms. The pieces of fabric were sewn together by hand to form clothing and table-cloths. These products quickly became popular throughout New England. Eventually, these linens even made their way back across the sea, for sale in England.

By the mid-1700s, several additional settlements were started by immigrants from Ulster. The Scotch-Irish had become important members of New Hampshire society.

John Wentworth

One of the most important families during this time in New Hampshire's history was the Wentworths. The Wentworth family contributed much to the growth and success of the colony. In 1717, the king of England appointed John Wentworth lieutenant governor of the New Hampshire colony. Members of the Wentworth family would rule in New Hampshire until 1775.

John Wentworth had grown up in the New Hampshire colony. He realized that the people of New Hampshire needed a leader who would work for them. His time in office marks the beginning of the colony's move toward establishing its own identity. He was the first lieutenant governor of New Hampshire to work without much help from the leaders of Massachusetts. While in office, Wentworth encouraged economic development. He also worked hard to settle boundary disputes between New Hampshire and Massachusetts in New Hampshire's favor.

John Wentworth died in 1730 while still in office. A historian described his time in office: "The administration of Lieutenant Governor Wentworth gave a dignified beginning to the administrative record of his family which covered so large a part of the 18th century in Portsmouth."

John Wentworth's son, Benning, believed that New Hampshire should once and for all break away from the control of Massachusetts. He felt that the colony should have an independent governor of its own. Benning Wentworth wanted very much to be that governor.

Deadly Disease

As the leadership of New Hampshire changed hands, life for the colonists continued to be a blend of hard work, struggle, and family life. But during the 1730s, family life was often shattered as disease spread throughout the colony. In several New Hampshire towns, between one-third and one-half of the children died of a powerful, highly contagious throat infection. Although there are no good medical records from the period, historians believe that the deadly disease was probably **diphtheria**. This disease still exists today, although not in the United States.

Benning Wentworth

In 1740, King George II of England settled an argument between Massachusetts and New Hampshire over some land. He granted twenty-eight towns and 3,500 square miles (9,100 square kilometers) of land that had once been part of Massachusetts to New Hampshire. As a result, New Hampshire grew greatly in size overnight. By 1741, the king felt that the colony had grown and prospered enough to have its own separate government. He made Benning Wentworth the first independent governor of New Hampshire. With that, New Hampshire once again became its own colony, breaking away from Massachusetts permanently.

Wentworth immediately built a mansion in Portsmouth. There, he lived like a king. He threw fancy parties. He issued land grants all over New Hampshire, mostly to his friends. Wentworth also cleverly kept 500 acres (200 hectares) from each grant for himself. He eventually owned over 100,000 acres (40,000 hectares) in the colony.

Vermont ★

One area in which Governor Benning Wentworth issued land grants became known as the New Hampshire Grants. New Hampshire found itself in conflict with New York over ownership of this land. The territory of the New Hampshire Grants eventually broke away and became Vermont. Vermont was the first state after the original thirteen colonies to later join the new United States of America.

New Hampshire Prospers

Benning Wentworth and his family grew wealthy during his term as governor. The New Hampshire colony prospered as well. Roads were built as land travel became more common. In 1761, a stagecoach route was created. It carried passengers between Portsmouth and Boston.

Mail Delivery

Mail was carried to the colonists by riders on horseback called "post riders." Post riders followed the main roads, then made their way through the forest along trails and bridle paths. Post riders did not leave the cities at regular times, but only when they had received enough mail to make the trip worthwhile. Faraway settlements therefore received mail only about once a month. The amount of mail delivered in all thirteen colonies in a typical year was less than the amount now delivered in New York City in a single day.

Post riders sometimes blew a horn to announce their arrival in colonial towns.

With the Wentworths as its leading family, Portsmouth grew into an important colonial port. It was soon the colony's shipping, cultural, and industrial center. Huge shipyards built vessels that sailed to the West Indies for trade. The captains of these ships grew wealthy. Soon the main streets of Portsmouth were lined with elegant mansions.

Portsmouth was also the home of New Hampshire's first newspaper, the *New Hampshire Gazette*, which was published starting in 1756. Daniel Fowle, its printer and editor, had arrived in Portsmouth from Boston. He had been jailed there for printing what authorities called "a seditious [treasonous] pamphlet." His writings on the need for freedom of the press were welcomed in New Hampshire. The state's motto—"Live Free or Die!"—appeared on the top of the front page of each issue of the paper. The *New Hampshire Gazette* is still published today and is the nation's oldest newspaper.

Read All About It

In addition to the news of the day, the *New Hampshire Gazette* contained poetry, advertisements for escaped slaves, and announcements of the arrivals of cargo and passenger ships. It also printed the governor's speeches, some news of Europe, local gossip, and essays on politics, morals, and religion. The paper was delivered in much the same way as newspapers are delivered today.

Family Life

The colony of New Hampshire went through much growth and change in the first seven decades of the 1700s. But one aspect of colonial life remained almost exactly the same. This was the roles played by each member of a family.

Husbands had total control over the actions of their wives, as did parents over their children. Women did not vote or participate in the town's business. They even sat apart from the men at church services.

A girl received far less formal education than a boy did. She was expected to act almost as a servant in the home until she got married after the age of twenty-one, as was the custom of the time. At that point, she began her adult life of serving in her husband's home.

The responsibility of sons was to work for their fathers, whether as merchants, farmers, or tradesmen, until the age of twenty-one. The eldest son in a family was also responsible for caring for his parents when they grew old. In exchange for this care, he received most of the family's property when his father died. This included the home, land, business, savings, and other possessions.

If a teenage son was unhappy at home, he had the option of leaving home and finding a job. This usually meant joining a sailing crew and heading out to sea or joining a military company in times of war. In a quote that shows parents' concerns about teenagers, an anonymous (unknown) New Hampshire colonist wrote in 1757, "Young people grow uncommonly loose, rude, vain, and ungoverned."

Boys learned to shoot at an early age. Most young men joined the colonial militia. Being a part of the militia taught them discipline and how to fight in a military unit.

Sometimes a young couple under the age of twenty-one could find a minister willing to marry them. They would elope against their parents' wishes. Because land was plentiful in New Hampshire, these couples were often able to set up households on their own land.

Peace...For Now

As families maintained the daily routines of colonial life, the threat of Indian attack was always present. The last two wars with the French and Indians took place during Benning Wentworth's term in office.

Finally, in 1760, the French surrendered to the English in Montreal, Canada. In 1763, a peace treaty was signed. After seventy-four years of off-and-on war, peace finally came to New Hampshire. With fear of Abenaki attacks finally over, New Hampshire soldiers returned to their farms and families, adding to the colony's growth.

Although New Hampshire achieved peace, prosperity, and stability under Benning Wentworth's administration (1741–1767), many people felt that he was just too greedy. The hardworking colonists resented his huge mansion, fancy parties, and the huge amount of land he took for himself. In 1767, under pressure from the Governor's Council, he was forced to resign. Wentworth was replaced by his nephew, John, who became the third Wentworth to serve as governor of the New Hampshire colony.

The period of peace that followed the end of the French and Indian War in 1763 would last just a few short years. The next war, however, would give birth to a new nation and change the world, too.

New Hampshire farms grew and prospered after the French and Indian Wars.

CHAPTER SIX

Bracing for War

✳✳✳✳✳✳✳✳✳✳✳✳✳✳✳✳✳✳✳✳✳✳✳✳✳✳✳✳✳✳✳✳✳

New Roads

When Governor John Wentworth took over from his Uncle Benning in 1767, the population of New Hampshire stood at about 53,000 people. Most of those residents were gathered in three areas: the east coast, along the Piscataqua River; the central Merrimack Valley, along the Merrimack River; and in the western Connecticut Valley, along the Connecticut River. The interior, or middle, of the colony was still mostly unsettled.

Wentworth was interested in developing the interior regions of the state. He traveled through the forests and met with the few hardy souls who lived in small settlements in the woods. He established a settlement on Lake Winnipesaukee, deep in the interior forest. This settlement was set up to study wildlife and develop farming techniques suitable for poor growing conditions.

❧ *Dartmouth College in Hanover became the center of higher education in New Hampshire.*

To help the settlement grow, Wentworth ordered the building of roads into the interior of the colony. These roads, which linked the remote settlements with New Hampshire's larger towns, led to increased trade within the colony.

Wentworth was also responsible for the establishment of New Hampshire's first college. In 1769, the governor gave 40,000 acres (16,000 hectares) in Hanover, a relatively new town in the western part of the colony, to Reverend Eleazar Wheelock. On this land Wheelock built a school to educate both young colonists and Native Americans. The school was named Dartmouth College. It eventually grew into one of the finest colleges in the United States.

Building Roads

During his time in office, Governor John Wentworth supervised the building of more than 200 miles (320 kilometers) of new roads. These opened up the interior of the New Hampshire colony. Because there was no motorized equipment at the time, the roads had to be smoothed out by hand, using shovels. Teams of oxen, dragging cutting blades behind them, chopped down rough road surfaces. Mud was then used as a final coating to smooth out the surface.

Unfair Taxes

John Wentworth's active role in promoting the growth of New Hampshire and the well-being of its colonists made him a popular governor. In addition, Wentworth was well liked by the king of England. For a while, Wentworth was able to balance the needs of the colonists with his loyalty to the king. This delicate balancing act got more and more difficult as the king began making stricter demands on the colonists.

The French and Indian War had cost England a lot of money. To raise money quickly, the British government began heavily taxing its colonies in America. Taxes on everyday items like tea and paper angered the colonists of New Hampshire and elsewhere.

The colonists were strong-willed, fair-minded people. They had always paid some taxes to help pay the cost of running the colony. But in return for paying those taxes, the colonists had a say in how the tax money was spent. But the colonists had no say in how the new taxes were spent. These taxes were sent directly to England. Decisions about how the tax money was used were made by the British government, which had no representatives from the colonies. "Taxation without representation is tyranny!" became the rallying cry of the angry colonists. This anger would grow with each new tax England imposed.

The Stamp Act

The town meeting had long been an important part of life in New Hampshire. Soon the colonists at the meetings were openly expressing their anger about the new taxes and laws imposed by the British.

In 1765, perhaps the most hated tax of all was imposed. The Stamp Act required colonists to buy stamps from the British government. These stamps had to be placed on legal documents and newspapers. Even playing cards had to have a stamp placed on them in order to be legal.

The Stamp Act required that printed materials have a government stamp like these before the items could be sold.

The colonists were furious about the Stamp Act. They demanded that it be repealed, or ended. A man named George Meserve was sent to Boston from England to collect this new tax in that city. Historian Jeremy Belknap in his *History of New Hampshire* details what happened: "Before he landed, he was informed of the opposition which was making to the act; and that it would be acceptable to the people [of the colonies] if he would resign, which he readily did, and they [the colonists] welcomed him on shore."

Anger Grows

Alarmed at the anger shown by the people of Boston, Meserve resigned as tax collector. He then headed to Portsmouth, New Hampshire, to perform his duties there. Met by an angry mob, Meserve quit once again. He never collected any money for the stamps he brought with him.

The Stamp Act had gone into effect in November 1765. By March 1766, the protests had become so widespread that the Stamp Act was repealed.

However, anger among the colonists of New Hampshire against the increased taxes and strict British laws continued to grow. Like the town meetings before them, the meetings of the New Hampshire Assembly turned into sessions at which members complained about the British. Many assembly members talked about rebelling, or fighting back, against the British.

Governor Wentworth tried to control the growing spirit of revolution by dissolving the New Hampshire Assembly. His plan did not work. New elections were held, and a new assembly was elected. The new assembly was even more rebellious.

As anger and dissatisfaction increased, the colony of New Hampshire moved closer and closer toward revolution. Times grew uncertain. The people were having a hard time paying the taxes imposed by England. But not all of the colonists were ready to break away from the mother country.

Colonists who supported the British were sometimes treated harshly by New Hampshire's citizens. Conflicts between Loyalists and Patriots increased as the British imposed more taxes.

The Church and the Town

In uncertain times, the colonists found a bit of security in everyday things. Family, church, and the community within a town formed the solid building blocks upon which day-to-day life continued.

A good deal of colonial life revolved around the church. Each town hired a minister. The minister led worship services. These were usually held twice on Sunday and once during the week. Church services also gave townspeople a chance to socialize. Many arrived early or stayed after the services to catch up on local news, discuss rumors of rebellion, or just to talk about the weather.

Another thing the local church provided was a way to punish those who did not stay within the colony's strict rules of behavior. For failing to respect and honor their parents, for example, children would be scolded in front of the congregation.

Churchgoers often collected money to help fellow colonists in times of trouble. Failed crops or the death of a milk-producing cow could send a farm family into economic ruin. Working as a community through the church, the people looked out for each other.

New Hampshire Towns

Colonial life was mostly based in towns, which met many of the colonists' basic needs. Towns provided a military center, where the men could more easily defend their families as a group, rather than as individuals. Towns provided a political structure. There, laws were established and local officials were selected to see that the business of the town was run in the best way for the community.

The church steeple was the most visible sight in many New Hampshire towns.

Living in a town gave its residents a sense of who they were. It also gave them a feeling of belonging and a steady routine. The towns of colonial New Hampshire came to be known as "peaceable kingdoms." The name suggested that life in New Hampshire's towns was peaceful.

The laws of each town provided guidelines for everyday life. The laws were written to meet the needs of each specific community. Ministers helped solve family arguments. Rules for voting and collecting taxes (for the town, not for England) were spelled out clearly, as were the responsibilities of town officials. Living peacefully within the structure provided by the family, the church, and the town helped the people of New Hampshire make their colony into a state.

The First Continental Congress

A major step in that transformation took place in 1774. Early in the year, Governor Wentworth did away with the New Hampshire Assembly for the second time. In response, the colonists elected a representative from each town to be part of a newly formed New Hampshire Provincial Congress. This congress met in Exeter to choose two representatives to attend a meeting of representatives from all the colonies. The larger meeting was called the First Continental Congress. It was to be held in Philadelphia in September.

The idea for the First Continental Congress came from Samuel Adams of Massachusetts and Benjamin Franklin of Pennsylvania. Both men were important leaders in their colonies. They felt that a meeting of representatives from all the colonies would allow them to express their growing unhappiness over the taxes and laws imposed by the British.

Fifty-six **delegates**, including Nathaniel Folsom and John Sullivan of New Hampshire, met in Philadelphia on September 5, 1774. They drafted a list of requests for fairer treatment, which was sent to King George III in England. They also agreed to meet again in the spring of 1775 if England refused to listen to their requests.

The King Reacts

Meanwhile, fearing an uprising in the colonies, King George sent troops to America to make sure that order was maintained. The troops, led by General Thomas Gage, arrived in Massachusetts in the fall of 1774.

Knowing that the harsh New England winter was coming soon, Gage searched for carpenters to build barracks (housing) for his soldiers. But the spirit of rebellion was especially strong in Massachusetts, and he could find no workers willing to do the job. General Gage turned to Governor Wentworth of New Hampshire for help. The governor secretly sent New Hampshire carpenters to

Massachusetts to build barracks for Gage's troops. Wentworth did his best to keep this a secret from the colonists. He knew that they would take this act as proof that he was more loyal to the king than to them. But the secret got out. As Wentworth expected, it enraged the colonists. This incident marked a turning point in the colonists' support of Wentworth. His term as royal governor would soon end.

In October 1774, King George ordered all shipments of gunpowder to the colonies to stop. He feared that the colonists might use the gunpowder against his soldiers. Within a few months, his worst fears would come true.

Media Mouthpiece

As in today's world of politics, newspapers expressed opinions about the day's important events. During the buildup to the American Revolution, the *New Hampshire Gazette* played an important role in spreading the spirit of rebellion among the colonists. A writer for the *Gazette* attended a meeting of the Provincial Congress at which Governor Wentworth spoke. The paper reported that the governor "had deprived the people from any share in their own government for near twelve months." The newspaper stated that Wentworth's unfair actions in the name of the king had brought about the destruction of the governor's once great popularity and power.

Fort William and Mary

On the afternoon of December 13, 1774, a Boston silver-smith and fiercely devoted **Patriot** named Paul Revere galloped into Portsmouth, New Hampshire. Revere had come with bad news. He told the colonists that two **regiments** of British soldiers were sailing to Portsmouth. They were coming to secure the gunpowder and weapons at a fort there called Fort William and Mary. The colonists of Portsmouth reacted quickly.

Patriot leader Paul Revere brought the news that the British were coming to capture Fort William and Mary.

The very next day, 400 colonists stormed Fort William and Mary. They easily overpowered the handful of British soldiers stationed there. They took guns, a cannon, and a hundred barrels of gunpowder and hid them in various places around the colony. The stolen weapons and ammunition were used five months later, when fighting against the British broke out in Massachusetts.

The raid on Fort William and Mary in New Hampshire is considered by most historians to be the first military act by the colonists against the British in the American Revolution. It took place four months before the battles at Lexington and Concord in Massachusetts. These battles signaled the official start of the War of Independence.

Both King George and Governor Wentworth of New Hampshire were outraged by the raid on Fort William and Mary. Wentworth ordered those who had participated in the raid arrested, but he did not have enough soldiers to carry out his orders. Wentworth's power in New Hampshire was quickly slipping away.

The War Begins

On April 20, 1775, news of the battles in Lexington and Concord, Massachusetts, reached New Hampshire. Men from various towns, including Portsmouth, Exeter, and Londonderry, went to fight. They were local townspeople, farmers and merchants, of all ages. One colonist said, "We all set out with what weapons we could get, going like a flock of wild geese, we hardly knew why or whither."

A colonist from New Ipswich, New Hampshire, described the soldiers and their lack of formal uniforms and weapons:

To a man, they wore long stockings with cowhide shoes ornamented by large buckles, while not a pair of boots graced the company. Their shirts were made of flax, and like every other part of the dress, were homespun. On their heads was worn a broad-brimmed hat. Their arms [weapons] were as various as their costume. Occasionally a bayonet [a sharp blade placed on the end of a rifle] might be seen bristling in the ranks. Some of the swords had been made by our Province blacksmiths, perhaps from some farming utensil. They looked serviceable, but heavy and uncouth [rough].

Two thousand New Hampshire men marched to Massachusetts to join their fellow Patriots in the war against England. They were led by Captain John Stark, a military leader and hero of the French and Indian War. Stark was the first to use the phrase that summed up the state's philosophy and became its official motto, "Live Free or Die!" Many of Stark's men were armed with weapons and gunpowder that had been taken during the raid on Fort William and Mary in 1774.

Patriot militiamen fought British soldiers at Lexington and Concord, Massachusetts. These battles launched the American Revolution.

The Spirit of Revolution

The original group of settlers that had come to New Hampshire more than a hundred years earlier considered themselves British. They were happy to settle the new land for the king and for England. Most colonists of the 1770s, however, did not consider themselves to be British. Most had never even been in England. They were born and raised in America. Their parents and grandparents had also been born and raised in America. They had little sense of loyalty to the mother country, especially when that country treated them unfairly.

In May 1775, the Provincial Congress of New Hampshire set up its own revolutionary government. It was revolutionary because it was opposed to the official government of the colonies, that of England. Setting up a new government like the Provincial Congress of New Hampshire was against the law. The Provincial Congress sent members of the New Hampshire militia to Massachusetts to aid the colonists there. More fighting between British soldiers (called redcoats because of the color of their uniforms) and colonial Patriots broke out a few months later.

The spirit of revolution spread from the Provincial Congress to colonists throughout New Hampshire. By

August 1775, anti-British feeling in New Hampshire was so strong that Governor John Wentworth was finally forced to leave office. He fled from the colony, never to return. The last colonial governor had left New Hampshire. This was the end of a British-controlled government in the colony.

When Wentworth left, the Provincial Congress officially took over as the government of New Hampshire. One of the first decisions it made was to change the word *colony* in all official documents to the word *state* to describe New Hampshire. A colony was a dependent part of Great Britain. A state was part of a separate country. The change in wording symbolized that New Hampshire was ready to join the other colonies as part of an independent nation.

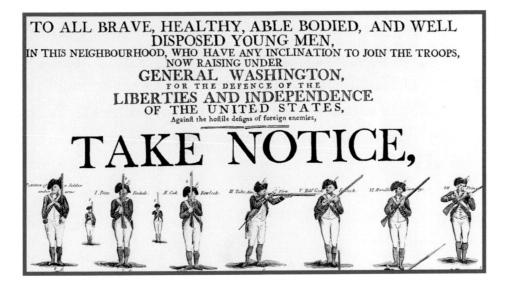

Posters like this recruited troops for the state militias and Patriot army.

The Declaration of Independence

On January 6, 1776, the Provincial Congress met in Exeter. There, the members wrote a state constitution. New Hampshire became the first of the thirteen colonies to create its own state constitution.

On June 15, the New Hampshire Declaration of Rights was adopted by the state congress. This document declared that New Hampshire was free of British rule. It also instructed the delegates from New Hampshire who were to attend the Continental Congress the following month to vote in favor of all thirteen colonies declaring their freedom from England.

On July 4, 1776, three delegates from New Hampshire joined those from the other colonies at the Second Continental Congress in Philadelphia. There they signed a national Declaration of Independence, announcing the birth of a new nation called the United States of America. With this declaration, the days of British rule in North America were over.

Seven more years of bloodshed and struggle were about to begin.

☛ *New Hampshire had its own Declaration of Rights which laid out the rights of its citizens and its plan for self-government.*

A DECLARATION

of RIGHTS, and PLAN of Government for the State of New-Hampſhire.

WHEREAS by the tyrannical Adminiſtration of the Government of the King and Parliament of Great-Britain, this State of New-Hampſhire, with the other United-States of AMERICA, have been neceſſitated to reject the Britiſh Government, and declare themſelves INDEPENDENT STATES ; all which is more largely ſet forth by the CONTINENTAL CONGRESS, in their Reſolution or Declaration of the fourth of July A. D. 1776.

AND WHEREAS, it is recommended by the ſaid CONTINENTAL CONGRESS to each and every of the ſaid United-States to eſtabliſh a FORM OF GOVERNMENT moſt conducive to the Welfare thereof. We the DELEGATES of the ſaid State of NEW-HAMPSHIRE choſen for the Purpoſe of forming a permanent PLAN of GOVERNMENT ſubject to the Reviſal of our CONSTITUENTS, have compoſed the following DECLARATION of RIGHTS, and PLAN of GOVERNMENT ; and recommend the ſame to our CONSTITUENTS for their Approbation.

A DECLARATION of the RIGHTS of the PEOPLE of the STATE of NEW-HAMPSHIRE.

Firſt, WE declare, that we the People of the State of New-Hampſhire, are Free and Independant of the Crown of Great-Britain.

Secondly. We the People of this State, are intitled to Life, Liberty, and Property ; and all other Immunities and Privileges which we heretofore enjoyed.

Thirdly. The Common and Statute Laws of England, adopted and uſed here, and the Laws of this State (not inconſiſtent with ſaid Declaration of INDEPENDENCE) now are, and ſhall be in force here, for the Welfare and good Government of the State, unleſs the ſame ſhall be repealed or altered by the future Legiſlature thereof.

Fourthly. The whole and intire Power of Government of this State, is veſted in, and muſt be derived from the People thereof, and from no other Source whatſoever.

Fifthly. The future Legiſlature of this State, ſhall make no Laws to infringe the Rights of Conſcience, or any other of the natural, unalienable Rights of Men, or contrary to the Laws of GOD, or againſt the Proteſtant Religion.

Sixthly. The Extent of Territory of this State, is, and ſhall be the ſame which was under the Government of the late Governor John Wentworth, Eſq; Governor of New-Hampſhire. Reſerving nevertheleſs, our Claim to the New-Hampſhire Grants, ſo called, ſituate to the Weſt of Connecticut River.

Seventhly. The Right of Trial by Jury in all Caſes as heretofore uſed in this State, ſhall be preſerved inviolate forever.

A PLAN of Government for the State of New-Hampſhire.

Firſt, THE State of New-Hampſhire ſhall be governed by a COUNCIL, and Houſe of REPRESENTATIVES, to be choſen as herein after mentioned, and to be ſtiled the GENERAL-COURT of the State of New-Hampſhire.

Second. The COUNCIL ſhall conſiſt for the preſent of twelve Members to be elected out of the ſeveral Counties in the State, in Proportion to their reſpective Number of Inhabitants.

Third. The Numbers belonging to each County for the preſent, according to ſaid Proportion being as followeth, viz.—To the County of Rockingham, five—to the County of Strafford, two---to the County of Hillſborough, two---to the County of Cheſhire, two---to the County of Grafton, one

Fourth. The number for the County of Rockingham, ſhall not be increaſed or diminiſhed hereafter, but remain the ſame ; and the Numbers for the other Counties ſhall be increaſed or deminiſhed as their aforeſaid Proportion to the County of Rockingham may chance to vary.

Fifth. The Houſe of REPRESENTATIVES ſhall be choſen as follows. Every Town or Pariſh, chooſing Town Officers, amounting to one hundred Families, and upwards, ſhall ſend one Repreſentative for each hundred Families they conſiſt of, (or ſuch leſſer Number as they pleaſe) or claſs themſelves with ſome other Towns or Pariſhes that will join in ſending a Repreſentative.

Sixth. All other Towns and Pariſhes under the number of one hundred Families, ſhall have Liberty to claſs themſelves together to make the number of one hundred Families or upwards, and being ſo claſſed, each Claſs ſhall ſend one Repreſentative.

Seventh. The number of COUNCILLORS belonging to each County ſhall be aſcertained and done by the General-Court every Time there is a new Proportion made of the State Tax which ſhall be once in ſeven Years at the leaſt, and oftner if need be.

Eighth. All the Male-Inhabitants of the State of lawful Age, paying Taxes, and profeſſing the Proteſtant Religion, ſhall be deemed legal Voters in chooſing COUNCILLORS and REPRESENTATIVES, and having an Eſtate of *Three Hundred Pounds* equal to Silver at ſix Shillings and eight Pence per Ounce, one half whereof to be real Eſtate, and lying within this State, with the Qualifications aforeſaid, ſhall be capable of being elected.

Ninth. The Selectmen of each reſpective Town and Pariſh, chooſing Town Officers containing one hundred Families or upwards, and alſo of each reſpective Claſs of Towns claſſed together as aforeſaid, ſhall notify the legal Voters of their reſpective Towns, Pariſhes, or Claſſes, qualified as aforeſaid, in the uſual Way of notifying Town-Meetings, giving fifteen Days notice at leaſt, to meet at ſome convenient Place on the laſt Wedneſday of November annually, to chooſe COUNCILLORS and REPRESENTATIVES.

Tenth. And the Voters being met, and the Moderator choſen, ſhall proceed to chooſe their Repreſentative or Repepreſentatives, required by this Conſtitution by a Majority of the Voters preſent, who ſhall be notified accordingly, and a Return thereof made into the Secretary's Office, by the firſt Wedneſday of January then next.

Eleventh. And ſuch Repreſentatives ſhall be paid their Wages by their Conſtituents, and for their Travel by the State.

Twelvth. And in the Choice of COUNCILLORS each Voter ſhall deliver his Vote to the Moderator for the number of COUNCILLORS reſpectively required, with the Word COUNCILLORS writen thereon, & the Voters Name endorſed to prevent Duplicity.

Thirteenth. Theſe Votes ſhall be ſealed up by the Moderator, and tranſmitted by the Conſtable to one of the Juſtices of the Inferior Court of Common Pleas for the County, before the ſecond Wedneſday in December next following.

CHAPTER SEVEN

The Revolutionary War

****

On July 4, 1776, the Declaration of Independence was signed in Philadelphia. The news of this event reached Portsmouth, New Hampshire, on July 18. People poured into the streets, shouting and celebrating. Caught up in the spirit of revolution, townspeople tore down street signs bearing the names of kings and queens of England. They threw stones at anything that displayed royal power, such as pictures and statues.

When the news arrived in Exeter, every man, woman, and child stopped what he or she was doing and quickly gathered in the center of town. A rider who came all the way from Philadelphia delivered a copy of the Declaration of Independence. The messenger read the declaration aloud. He had to pause several times because he was overcome with emotion. The people of Exeter reacted with feelings of joy, relief, and hope for a better future.

Fifteen hundred New Hampshire militiamen defeated British forces at the Battle of Bennington in Vermont.

The signing of the Declaration of Independence marked the beginning of the War of Independence, also called the Revolutionary War. No battles were fought in New Hampshire during the Revolutionary War. It was the only one of the original thirteen colonies where fighting did not take place.

However, the people of New Hampshire did play an important role in the war for independence from England. Trained soldiers, farmers, blacksmiths, shoemakers, and other Patriots rushed to the battlefields of Massachusetts, New York, New Jersey, Rhode Island, Pennsylvania, and Virginia. Soldiers from New Hampshire took part in every major battle. By the time the Revolutionary War ended, roughly 5,000 men from New Hampshire had fought against the British.

The government of the New Hampshire colony was moved out of Portsmouth to the much smaller inland town of Exeter for safety. As a port city, Portsmouth was in danger of being attacked from the sea by the powerful British navy.

Portsmouth During the War

As the war went on, Portsmouth began to play an important role in the fight of the United States against the British. Portsmouth was home to many privateers, owners of private ships used by the government to fight naval battles.

These ships, manned by close to 3,000 New Hampshire residents, patrolled the coastline. They battled the British navy and seized or destroyed some of its ships. As a reward for their efforts, the sailors who worked on the privateers shared in the profits from whatever cargo was taken. Many got rich. Many others were captured or killed.

PRIVATEERS VS. THE CONTINENTAL NAVY

A look at the numbers, comparing the ships in America's Continental navy to the hired privateers, shows how big a role these private ships played in America's victory over England:

	CONTINENTAL NAVY	PRIVATEERS
Total number of ships	64	1,697
Total number of guns on the ships	1,246	14,872
Number of enemy ships captured	196	2,283

The Portsmouth shipyards also helped in the war by building three great warships for the newly formed Continental navy. These were the *Raleigh*, the *America*, and the *Ranger*. The *Ranger*, commanded by naval hero John Paul Jones, was the first warship to fly the brand-new American flag.

Wealthy New Hampshire merchants who lived and ran their businesses along the coast suffered economic disaster during the war. Since there were so many warships around, there was almost no trade by sea. On the other hand, farmers did well growing food to feed the troops. The population of New Hampshire actually increased during the war years, possibly because the region seemed safe compared to colonies where there was more fighting going on. By the time the war ended, close to 95,000 people lived in the state.

The War Ends

The final battle of the Revolutionary War took place in Yorktown, Virginia. In September 1781, General George Washington and his army of 17,000 soldiers, including many from New Hampshire, confronted and defeated the British in Yorktown. On October 19, 1781, British general Charles Cornwallis surrendered to Washington. The bloody fighting was over.

The war that made the colonies into free states independent from England officially ended on September 3, 1783. On that day, representatives of the United States and England met in Paris, France, to sign a formal peace treaty. The people of New Hampshire celebrated. They gathered in their local meetinghouses to offer thanks for the end of the war and for their freedom. At night, fireworks exploded in the sky above crowds of cheering people.

Years of war, hardship, destruction, and death had ended. New Hampshire and the twelve other former colonies now faced the task of becoming a nation.

The Surrender

When British general Cornwallis realized that he no longer had a chance of victory, he sent a message to General Washington. Cornwallis requested a twenty-four-hour cease-fire during which he asked Washington to draw up his terms for the surrender of the British. Washington worked through the night writing up the articles of surrender. At eleven o'clock the following morning, Cornwallis signed the agreement, ending the war.

CHAPTER EIGHT

Statehood

✶✶✶✶✶✶✶✶✶✶✶✶✶✶✶✶✶✶✶✶✶✶✶✶✶✶✶✶✶✶✶

The end of the Revolutionary War brought great celebrations in the towns of New Hampshire. The people were relieved to be free of both British rule and the war itself. Along with their freedom, however, came great responsibility. No longer could the former colonies turn to royal governors, the ruler of England, or the British government for guidance. The new states would have to form a government of their own whose laws, rules, and systems would serve the needs of all Americans. The leaders of the new nation willingly accepted the challenge.

New Hampshire had drafted and adopted its own state constitution in 1776. This document had been written quickly and put into effect without any input from the people of the state. In 1778, the citizens of New Hampshire demanded that their state constitution be rewritten. They wanted a chance to vote on its approval. Over the next six years, the state constitution was rewritten and voted upon

After the Revolutionary War, soldiers collected their pay and left the army. They returned to their farms and trades in the new United States.

three times. Finally, on July 1, 1784, the constitution was approved. More than 220 years later, this same state constitution still governs the people of New Hampshire.

The Constitutional Convention

By 1787 it was clear that a national constitution was needed. In May of that year, the Constitutional Convention was held in Philadelphia. The purpose of this convention was to write a national constitution outlining how the United States would be governed, and the rights of its people.

New Hampshire sent two delegates to the Constitutional Convention to represent the state. They were John Langdon and Nicholas Gilman. Langdon, who had helped lead the raid on Fort William and Mary, would become the first U.S. senator from New Hampshire. Gilman was active in state politics and would go on to serve four terms in New Hampshire's House of Representatives.

Along with delegates from the other states (except for Rhode Island, which did not send any delegates), Langdon and Gilman helped write the Constitution of the United States. By early 1788, the new Constitution was ready. It then needed to be **ratified** (approved) by the individual states in order to be put into effect. The convention decided that if two-thirds of the states (nine states) approved the document, it would become the law of the land.

Many people in New Hampshire were not sure they wanted to approve the U.S. Constitution. They believed that state control was better than the control of a national, or federal, government. They were worried that a federal government located far away would not look after the interests of their small state.

There was much debate among the delegates who met to vote on whether New Hampshire should ratify the Constitution. Eight other states had already voted to accept the document. Finally, on June 21, 1788, the New Hampshire delegates voted 57–47 in favor of the Constitution. As the ninth state to ratify the Constitution, New Hampshire's vote made it official. The Constitution was adopted and was now the law of the United States.

When word of the ratification reached Portsmouth, a huge parade took place. New Hampshire residents from all walks of life came out to celebrate. Farmers, tradesmen, and town officials marched together through the streets.

New Hampshire Firsts

Today, New Hampshire is known as the "first in the nation," because it holds the first presidential primary. Here are other New Hampshire firsts:

• In 1719, the first potato in America was planted at Londonderry Common Field.

• In 1767, the first summer resort in America opened at the summer home of Royal Governor John Wentworth in Wolfeboro, New Hampshire.

• In 1833, the first free public library in America opened in Peterborough, New Hampshire.

The Growth of a State

Despite this excitement, times were tough in the years immediately after the Revolution. The cost of the war left New Hampshire in debt. There had been no foreign trade during the war years. This hurt merchants and other workers in Portsmouth. By the 1790s, though, things began to improve. As trade increased, money and jobs flowed into the town.

Mills powered by waterwheels were a common sight along New Hampshire's many rivers and streams.

Before and during the Revolutionary War, each colony issued its own money. This five-shilling bill would be worth about fifteen dollars in today's money.

In the early part of the 1800s, industry grew all over the state. Cotton mills (in which thread was woven into fabric on power looms) and other factories sprang up. These factories were powered by waterwheels in New Hampshire's swiftly flowing streams.

The western part of the state, long overlooked, was now being settled. The population of the region grew quickly in the early years of the nineteenth century. In 1808, the state capital was moved from Portsmouth to Concord, an inland town on the Merrimack River.

Industry and manufacturing grew. But in the early years of its statehood, the main occupation in New Hampshire was still farming. The farmer's life had always been difficult.

Most farmwork was done using hand tools and the power of the farmer's own back, arms, and legs. Horses and oxen were used to move heavy loads and pull plows. Tall grass was cut to create hay to feed the animals. Firewood was cut using an axe. Farm chores had to be done in the heat of the summer and the frozen days of winter.

Farm Families

Women worked just as hard as men did. The average New Hampshire family in the early days of statehood consisted of a father, mother, and four or five children. Women were responsible for cooking, cleaning, and feeding the six or seven people in the home. They also tended crops, picked fruits and berries, spun wool into thread, and made butter in a hand-operated churn. It was not unusual for a farm woman to ride a horse 60 or 70 miles (96 or 112 kilometers) from her farm to the nearest big town to sell the butter. She might carry two 50-pound (22.5-kilogram) tubs of butter placed in bags and slung over her horse's back.

Farm families did not have much money. Instead of using money, they traded with others for items or services they needed. For example, a farmer might take some turnips or squash and five calves to a neighbor's house. The neighbor would kill the calves, remove the skins, and dress (prepare) the meat. As payment for this service, the neighbor would take the vegetables, returning the calf meat and skins to the farmer. The farmer would then bring the skins and a bushel of wheat to another neighbor, who would tan the skins in exchange for the wheat. Tanning the animals' skin turned it into leather.

Butter was made by churning cream in barrels or large clay pots. It took thirty to sixty minutes of churning to make butter.

Next, a traveling shoemaker would arrive and live at the farmer's house for several days while making the leather into shoes for the farmer's family. In payment, the farmer might build a wooden yoke (harness), which the shoemaker then used to attach an ox to a cart in order to carry heavy loads.

This exchange of skills and goods formed the rhythm of everyday life for most of the people in New Hampshire. Writer Nathaniel Holmes, the grandson of a Peterborough, New Hampshire, farmer, wrote about life on his grand-father's farm in the early part of the 1800s:

Two or three hundred acres of forest had been brought into conditions of a well ordered farm with a due proportion of arable fields [good for planting and growing], meadows, pastures, orchards and woodlands. Several miles of stone walls had been built and the large barns were filled with hay and grain. One cellar was filled from ground to ceiling with potatoes, another with hogs heads [large barrels] of cider, leaving scarcely room for the apple bins, much frequented by boys and girls going to school. Another [cellar] was [used for] dairy, which occupied all the women in the house. And the cheese safe contained long rows of cheese, well ripened. Butter was salted in firkins [small wooden containers]. The surplus of course were articles for market, and one or more trips were made each year to Boston, sixty miles off.

This tough, determined, **self-sufficient** attitude among its residents, still present today, helped New Hampshire grow as a state and as part of a new nation.

New Hampshire's dairy farms grew after the Revolution. New Hampshire became an important supplier of dairy products to the new nation.

Recipe
Succotash

The early settlers of New Hampshire learned how to make this mixture of corn and beans from the Indians. The natives often added other vegetables from their farms, meat, or fowl. They sometimes seasoned the dish with bear fat. The settlers stuck with just the beans and corn.

Modern Version

2 tablespoons butter
1 cup whole kernel corn
1 cup lima beans
1/2 cup broth or cream

- Melt butter in a saucepan over medium heat.

- Sauté the corn in the butter until it begins to brown.

- Add the remaining ingredients and simmer until tender, 15–20 minutes.

- Add salt and pepper to taste.

NOTE: *This recipe works best with fresh corn cut from the cob (which is what the Native Americans and colonists used), but canned corn can be used, as well.*

This activity should be done with adult supervision.

Activity
Cup and Ball Game

Children living in colonial times often made their own toys. The cup and ball toy was a favorite plaything. The object of this game was to toss a ball into the air and catch it in the cup. The cup was made from wood and had a wooden or clay ball attached to it by a string. To get the ball into the cup, your eyes and hand had to work together. The cup and ball game is not as simple as it looks. It takes patience and concentration to be successful. Try it!

Directions

*Paper or plastic cup • Hole-punch
Pencil • 18-inch piece of string or yarn
Duct, masking, or clear plastic tape
Large sheet of aluminum foil*

- Punch or poke a hole in the side of the cup, about 1/2 inch from the top.

- Tape the pencil to the outside of the cup so that the end of the pencil extends below the bottom of the cup.

- Thread yarn or string through the hole in the side of the cup. Make a tight knot. Tape the string to the inside of the cup if necessary.

- Place the other end of the string in the middle of the sheet of aluminum foil.

- Wrap the foil around the yarn or string several times and then make a ball with the foil. The ball should be smaller than the mouth of the cup.

- The string should attach the foil ball to the top of the cup.

- To play the game, place the ball in the cup. Then, toss the ball into the air. Try to catch it in the cup.

Good luck!

This activity should be done with adult supervision.

NEW HAMPSHIRE
Time Line

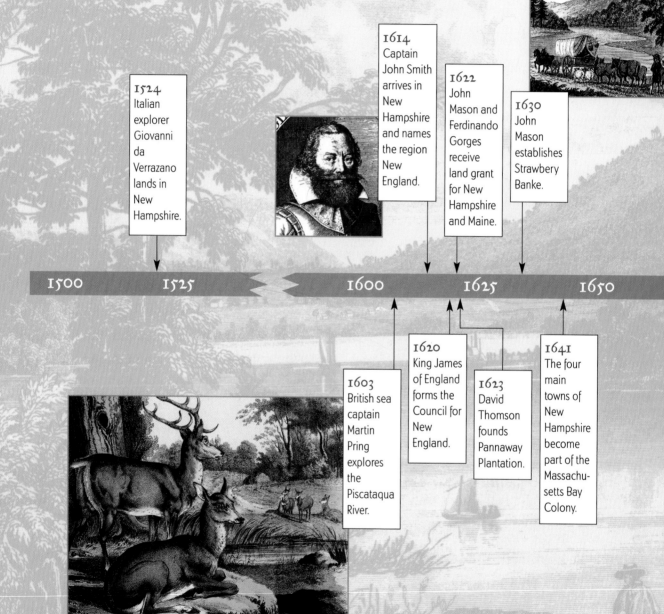

1524
Italian explorer Giovanni da Verrazano lands in New Hampshire.

1614
Captain John Smith arrives in New Hampshire and names the region New England.

1622
John Mason and Ferdinando Gorges receive land grant for New Hampshire and Maine.

1630
John Mason establishes Strawbery Banke.

1500   **1525**   **1600**   **1625**   **1650**

1603
British sea captain Martin Pring explores the Piscataqua River.

1620
King James of England forms the Council for New England.

1623
David Thomson founds Pannaway Plantation.

1641
The four main towns of New Hampshire become part of the Massachusetts Bay Colony.

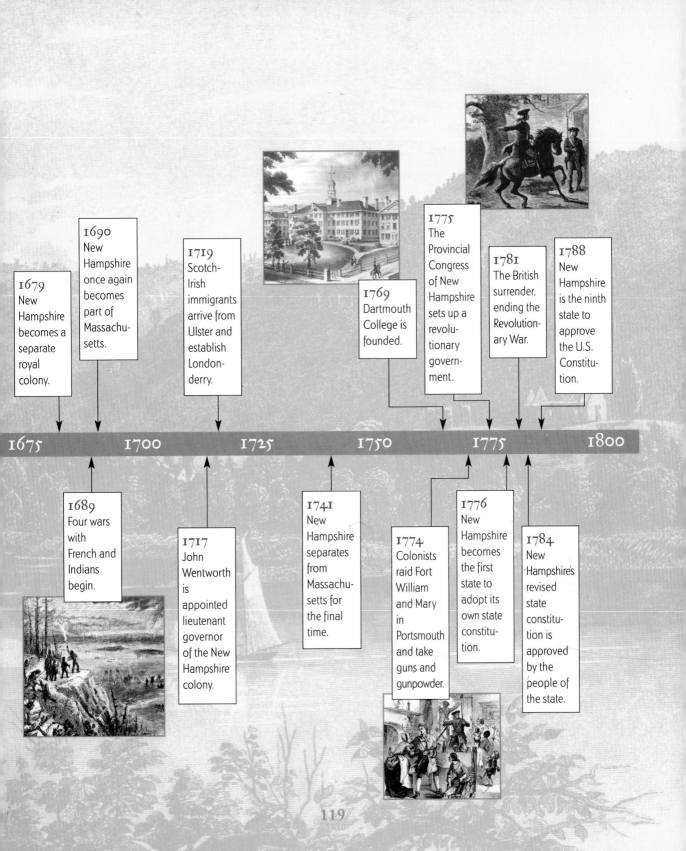

1679
New Hampshire becomes a separate royal colony.

1690
New Hampshire once again becomes part of Massachusetts.

1719
Scotch-Irish immigrants arrive from Ulster and establish Londonderry.

1769
Dartmouth College is founded.

1775
The Provincial Congress of New Hampshire sets up a revolutionary government.

1781
The British surrender, ending the Revolutionary War.

1788
New Hampshire is the ninth state to approve the U.S. Constitution.

1675   1700   1725   1750   1775   1800

1689
Four wars with French and Indians begin.

1717
John Wentworth is appointed lieutenant governor of the New Hampshire colony.

1741
New Hampshire separates from Massachusetts for the final time.

1774
Colonists raid Fort William and Mary in Portsmouth and take guns and gunpowder.

1776
New Hampshire becomes the first state to adopt its own state constitution.

1784
New Hampshire's revised state constitution is approved by the people of the state.

Further Reading

****

Blohm, Craig E. *The Thirteen Colonies: New Hampshire.* San Diego: Lucent Books, 2002.

Daniel, Jere R. *Colonial New Hampshire.* Millwood, NY: KTO Press, 1981.

Davis, Kevin A. *The New Hampshire Colony.* Chanhassen, MN: Child's World, 2003.

Jager, Ronald, and Grace Jager. *New Hampshire: An Illustrated History of the Granite State.* Woodland Hills, CA: Windsor Publications, 1983.

Whitehurst, Susan. *The Colony of New Hampshire.* New York: Powerkids Press, 2001.

Glossary

✳✳✳✳✳✳✳✳✳✳✳✳✳✳✳✳✳✳✳✳✳✳✳✳✳✳✳✳✳✳✳✳✳✳✳✳

churn to agitate or stir milk or cream in order to make butter; also the container that holds the milk

delegate a representative sent to a meeting by a group of people to express their views

diphtheria an often deadly disease that attacks the throat, tonsils, and nose

embroidery a type of ornamental needlework, using thread sewn into cloth

expedition a journey whose purpose is exploration

grant a legal document giving someone ownership of a piece of land

impose to force someone to accept something

mast a pole on a sailing ship, from which the sails are hung

migration the movement of a group of people from one locality to another

militia an army made up of ordinary citizens instead of professional soldiers nomads groups of people with no established homes, who travel from place to place in search of food

Patriot in the American Revolution, someone who sided with the colonists fighting the British

portable easily carried or moved

ratify to approve by a formal agreement

regiment a military unit consisting of several hundred soldiers

sachem a chief of an Algonquian tribe

self-sufficient able to do things without help

tendon the tough tissue that connects muscles and bones in animals

till to plow or otherwise prepare land for raising crops

tradesman a craftsman engaged in making and selling goods

treaty a formal peace or trade agreement between two or more nations

wigwam a dome-shaped Indian dwelling covered with tree bark or animal hides

Index

✳✳✳✳✳✳✳✳✳✳✳✳✳✳✳✳✳✳✳✳✳✳✳✳✳✳✳✳✳✳✳✳✳✳✳